The Effects of Knut Hamsun
on a Fresno Boy

Other Books by Gary Soto

THE EFFECTS OF KNUT HAMSUN ON A FRESNO BOY

Recollections and Short Essays

BY GARY SOTO

A Karen and Michael Braziller Book
PERSEA BOOKS / NEW YORK

Persea Books, Inc.
853 Broadway
New York, NY 10003

Library of Congress Cataloging-in-Publication Data

Soto, Gary
   The effects of Knut Hamsun on a Fresno boy : recollections and short essays / by Gary Soto.—1st. ed.
   p. cm.
ISBN 0-89255-254-9 (pbk. : alk. paper)
   1. Soto, Gary. 2. Poets, American—20th century—Biography. 3. Fresno (Calif.)—Biography. I. Title.

PS3569.072.Z465 2000
811'.54—dc21
[B]   00-062430
Manufactured in the United States of America
Second printing

To Carolyn, once again

CONTENTS

PREFACE

FOR ME, STREETS HAVE MATTERED. WHEN I AM READY TO write, ready to sit down, usually at the kitchen table but also in bed, I conjure up inside my head an image of our old street in south Fresno, where, at the beginning of the 1960s, house after house was torn down in the name of "urban renewal." There was, as one might imagine, a blighted junk-yard to the left of our house, Coleman Pickles across the street, a broom factory with its nightly *whack-whack* of machinery down the alley, and the almighty Sun-Maid Raisin factory in the distance. There were also weed-choked vacant lots where orange cats wandered cautiously and gophers burrowed holes large enough for a child to push his fist in, which I did.

The other Fresno streets also mattered, streets with names like Thomas and Grant, leading to simple family homes where sprinklers twirled on lawns and cooking smells wafted from open windows. I played every kind of game on these front lawns, and at night chewed stalks of grass under the immense window of the night sky. There, I thought about my life, the past, saying to my twelve-year-old self, "Gosh, wasn't eleven-and-a-half a great time?" I reflected on the incre-mental loss of years but did nothing about these feelings, except to share them with the sky that was wide and dark and amazingly endless. I chewed on stalks of grass and, a poet at heart at that young age, began to walk the meager streets, nose twitching from the smells of leaf fires or orange blossoms loosed on the wind. Mindlessly walking, I picked up so much of the arrangement of the world, both the large and the small that even to this day I can see a broken RC Cola bottle and recall my contemplating whether the bottle was full, half-full, or empty when it fell to the ground. This might be described as wonderment, I suppose.

Years later, the corner of Van Ness and Divisadero also mattered because that was where I came into my own as a young writer. In the summer of 1977, the year my first book of poems, *The Elements of San Joaquin,* appeared, my wife and I lived in a downtown cottage apartment, and I was very much following in the footsteps of Knut Hamsun, my favorite writer at the time and one who still ranks up there for me. Like Norwegian-born Hamsun, I was living through a writer's hunger not only for bread but also for words that would rise like leaven and feed my neighbors. While my wife was off at her job, I stayed indoors, hidden in the shadows where coolness dwelled until the sun shifted and rode fiercely through the front window. Outside, the heat squeezed moisture from every living hole on a body that ventured foolishly out at noon. But smarty me, I lurked in the shadows of our small bedroom where I wrote poems and stories and thought of Hamsun, poor writer himself, and how he drank his water and examined his hands, flighty birds that rested in his palms when they were not busy holding a pencil. He had only words to offer to the world, and the world, busy with commerce, offered only silence in return.

I assumed his life where he had left off and in my unemployed leisure replicated his steps not in cool and windy Norway but in hell-blazing Fresno. I walked around the neighborhood and picked up the sights that later became the material for my mature poetry and, still later, the short recollections and essays that make up this collection. As you will see, this is a collection of family and friends, of new places and old, and of my belief that wherever we stand—in my case, shoulder to shoulder with the kindred spirit of a long-dead writer—is where we belong. It's a collection that brings together all of my previously published volume, *Small Faces,* and a good portion of *Lesser Evils,* two books long out of print. Moreover, there are five new pieces, two of which are about the writing life.

And where did Mr. Hamsun go? Earthward, I believe. And where did that Fresno boy go after he started off with a pencil in one hand and lined paper in the other? Up and down, but mostly straight ahead, ant-like, carrying a story in his jaw.

ONE

The Girl on the Can of Peas

MY FIRST LOVE? I WAS FIVE AND SITTING IN OUR DIRT
yard on Braly Street. My brother Rick was hanging by almighty
luck in the almond tree and making bomb sounds. He flicked
unripe almonds at me, calling me names, but I didn't turn
around or get mad because I was mesmerized by the girl on
the can of peas, which I had pulled out of the garbage. I had
also taken out a milk carton, a soup can, a tuna can, and was
assembling them into a city that I intended to burn with
matches.

The girl possessed a flushed face, blond curls, a dance of
light in her eyes, which were looking right at me and had me
feeling embarrassed because I had spikey hair and sticky peach
stains at the corners of my mouth. I peeled the label off the
can and ran up the brick steps into the house to hide it, and
in my room I stared at her with a longing that was new to me.
But in time I returned outside, worn out from the deep feelings I had shared with her, and played soldiers with Rick.
Later we wandered into the alley to look for fruit—plums and
peaches—and found both in the yard of a Japanese family,
whose grandpa chased us with a rake all the way to the railroad
tracks at Van Ness Avenue. But he stopped there and just
swore. We walked up onto the tracks where we set rocks on the
oily rails and waited to see what would happen when a train
passed. When one did arrive in the distance, slow as a cloud,
we hid behind a telephone pole, no doubt visible to everyone,
feeling giddy that a train wreck was going to take place in our
young lives. We held our breath as its black shadow
approached and the engine roared in our chests. But not
much happened. Sparks flowered and snapped when the

wheels struck the rocks, which were kicked away and at once mingled with other rocks.

On the way home we sneaked past the Japanese yard where we heard the chatter of mad voices. In the kitchen we heated tortillas, smeared them with a knife blade of butter, and rolled them into fat flutes. We took them to our bedroom, which was a converted sun porch, and ate them. A vein of melted butter ran down my forearm to my elbow but I didn't care. I was happy, so happy that I showed Rick the label of the girl on the can of peas. He held it in his small hands like a treasure map and together we went dreamy with her beauty.

Rick asked where I had found it. I pointed to the alley and said a garbage can. Rick's face brightened up. "I know where she lives," he said. I looked at him dumbfounded because I couldn't imagine that someone so delicate and rich would live near a poor street like ours. He told me she lived only two or three blocks away. Together we went outside, up the alley like a couple of quiet cats, past the broom factory and the *whamwham* of its machinery, to the street our mother warned us never to cross. "She lives over there," Rick pointed. I looked and saw only a line of diesel trucks, vacant lots, brick buildings humming with work, but no houses where she might live.

"No sir,' I said with a screwed-up face, being no one's fool.

"Not there, stupid!" he snapped, "three streets from there. That's where the rich got their houses. They got the trucks parked there 'cause they don't want to see us."

It sounded plausible to me, but still I was scared of mother and her warning never to cross the street. I stood on the curb, my arms limp as wings, wanting to cross because the street didn't seem that scary. I could run over there, I thought, and be back in a flash. I bit my lip and begged Rick to come along. When he shook his head no, I stepped hesitantly from the curb, looking both ways, and then scurried like a rabbit across the street. I was breathless. I looked back at Rick who, with cupped hands, was yelling that I was a dead boy on the floor when mother found out. "He's a stupid Mexican," I said to myself, scared and almost crying as I watched Rick disappear up the alley on the way home where he would wait on the front porch for mother to return from Redi-Spud.

I walked past those diesels only to find another yard of diesels, and rusty buildings, a tire company. After a while I was so lost and confused at not finding the girl on the can of peas that I just sat down and cried into my arms.

How did I get back? I don't know, except I remember later that spring my cat Boots crossed that street, black asphalt snake of misfortune, and returned home with a sliver of wood in her eye. She died the next day, but her face, twisted with pain, stayed in my memory for years, long after I had lost that label of the girl on the can of peas.

The Jacket

MY CLOTHES HAVE FAILED ME. I REMEMBER THE GREEN coat that I wore in fifth and sixth grades when you either danced like a champ or pressed yourself against a greasy wall, bitter as a penny toward the happy couples.

When I needed a new jacket and my mother asked what kind I wanted, I described something like bikers wear: black leather and silver studs with enough belts to hold down a small town. We were in the kitchen, steam on the windows from her cooking. She listened so long while stirring dinner that I thought she understood for sure the kind I wanted. The next day when I got home from school, I discovered draped on my bedpost a jacket the color of day-old-guacamole. I threw my books on the bed and approached the jacket slowly, as if it were a stranger whose hand I had to shake. I touched the vinyl sleeve, the collar, and peeked at the mustard-colored lining.

From the kitchen mother yelled that my jacket was in the closet. I closed the door to her voice and pulled at the rack of clothes in the closet, hoping the jacket on the bedpost wasn't for me but my mean brother. No luck. I gave up. From my bed, I stared at the jacket. I wanted to cry because it was so ugly and so big that I knew I'd have to wear it a long time. I was a small kid, thin as a young tree, and it would be years before I'd have a new one. I stared at the jacket, like an enemy, thinking bad things before I took off my old jacket whose sleeves climbed halfway to my elbow.

I put the big jacket on. I zipped it up and down several times, and rolled the cuffs up so they didn't cover my hands. I put my hands in the pockets and flapped the jacket like a bird's wings. I stood in front of the mirror, full face, then profile, and then looked over my shoulder as if someone had called me. I sat on the bed, stood against the bed, and combed my hair to see what I would look like doing something natural. I looked ugly. I threw it on my brother's bed and looked at it for a long time before I slipped it on and went out to the backyard, smiling a "thank you" to my mom as I passed her in the kitchen. With my hands in my pockets I kicked a ball against the fence, and then climbed it to sit looking into the alley. I hurled orange peels at the mouth of an open garbage can and when the peels were gone I watched the white puffs of my breath thin to nothing.

I jumped down, hands in my pockets, and in the backyard on my knees I teased my dog, Brownie, by swooping my arms while making bird calls. He jumped at me and missed. He jumped again and again, until a tooth sunk deep, ripping an L-shaped tear on my left sleeve. I pushed Brownie away to study the tear as I would a cut on my arm. There was no blood, only a few loose pieces of fuzz. Damn dog, I thought, and pushed him away hard when he tried to bite again. I got up from my knees and went to my bedroom to sit with my jacket on my lap, with the lights out.

That was the first afternoon with my new jacket. The next day I wore it to sixth grade and got a D on a math quiz. During the morning recess Frankie T., the playground terrorist, pushed me to the ground and told me to stay there until recess was over. My best friend, Steve Negrete, ate an apple while looking at me, and the girls turned away to whisper on the monkey bars. The teachers were no help: they looked my way and talked about how foolish I looked in my new jacket. I saw their heads bob with laughter, their hands half-covering their mouths.

Even though it was cold, I took off the jacket during lunch and played kickball in a thin shirt, my arm feeling like braille from the goose bumps. But when I returned to class I slipped the jacket on and shivered until I was warm. I sat on my hands, heating them up, while my teeth chattered like a cup of crooked dice. Finally warm, I slid out of the jacket but a few minutes later put it back on when the fire bell rang. We paraded out into the yard where we, the sixth graders, walked past all the other grades to stand against the back fence. Everybody saw me. Although they didn't say out loud, "Man, that's ugly," I heard the buzz-buzz of gossip and even laughter that I knew was meant for me.

And so I went, in my guacamole-colored jacket. So embarrassed, so hurt, I couldn't even do my homework. I received Cs on quizzes, and forgot the state capitals and rivers of South America, our friendly neighbor. Even the girls who had been friendly blew away like loose flowers to follow the boys in neat jackets.

I wore that thing for three years until the sleeves grew short and my forearms stuck out like the necks of turtles. All during that time no love came to me—no little dark girl in a Sunday dress she wore on Monday. At lunchtime I stayed with the ugly boys who leaned against the chainlink fence and looked around with propellers of grass spinning in our mouths. We saw girls walk by alone, saw couples, hand in hand, their heads like bookends pressing air together. We saw them and spun our propellers so fast our faces were blurs.

I blame that jacket for those bad years. I blame my mother for her bad taste and her cheap ways. It was a sad time for the heart. With a friend I spent my sixth-grade year in a tree in the alley, waiting for something good to happen to me in that jacket, which had become the ugly brother who tagged along wherever I went. And it was about that time that I began to grow. My chest puffed up with muscle and, strangely, a few more ribs. Even my hands, those fleshy hammers, showed bravely through the cuffs, the fingers already hardening for the coming fights. But that L-shaped rip on the left sleeve got bigger, bits of stuffing coughed out from its wound after a hard day of play. I finally Scotch-taped it closed, but in rain or cold weather the tape peeled off like a scab and more stuffing fell out until that sleeve shriveled into a palsied arm. That winter the elbows began to crack and whole chunks of green began to fall off. I showed the cracks to my mother, who always seemed to be at the stove with steamed-up glasses, and she said that there were children in Mexico who would love that jacket. I told her that this was America and yelled that Debbie, my sister, didn't have a jacket like mine. I ran outside, ready to cry, and climbed the tree by the alley to think bad thoughts and watch my breath puff white and disappear.

But whole pieces still casually flew off my jacket when I played hard, read quietly, or took vicious spelling tests at school. When it became so spotted that my brother began to call me "camouflage," I flung it over the fence into the alley. Later, however, I swiped the jacket off the ground and went inside to drape it across my lap and mope.

I was called to dinner: steam silvered my mother's glasses as she said grace; my brother and sister with their heads bowed made ugly faces at their glasses of powdered milk. I gagged too, but eagerly ate big rips of buttered tortilla that held scooped-up beans. Finished, I went outside with my jacket across my arm. It was a cold sky. The faces of clouds were piled up, hurting. I climbed the fence, jumping down with a grunt. I started up the alley and soon slipped into my jacket, that green ugly brother who breathed over my shoulder that day and ever since.

The Arts

I'VE ALWAYS BEEN AMAZED BY WHAT OTHER PEOPLE CAN DO with watercolors and a sheet of paper because I've known for years that I wasn't meant for the arts. In first grade I drew a car and the teacher, a kind one with a warm hand, said, "Nice house, Gary." I drew houses and she declared, with her hands jumping to her breast, "Oh my, the Golden Hind!" I drew people whose faces looked like lopsided toasters, and dogs that resembled Tyrannosaurus Rex on a leash. The hats were clouds, and the clouds were bushes, and what looked like a length of fence was really my brother and sister holding hands.

I loved drawing nevertheless. I could see what I was doing. The fort was a fort, the people on horses were Indians, and the ones with rifles were soldiers. At my work bench I moved my crayon back and forth as I made this and that. I studied the drawing with my mouth half open in full admiration and then, very quietly at first, scribbled flames that picked up speed like a real fire.

The houses that looked like cars burned; the bushes that were clouds went up in flame. Hot fire poked around rich families, boats, and hungry dogs. While I drew I made the sound of a race car, even after the teacher shushed me with a finger pressed to her puckered mouth. I went silent but the car noise raced inside my head at a ferocious speed.

I've always admired the beauty of art because, in a way, it suggests the beauty in us, or, as Wallace Stevens put it, "the voice that is great within us." I've also enjoyed singing even though I couldn't sing to save a poodle's life. In kindergarten I sang "Banana Boat." A deep longing rose from my heart when I yelled "It's a day, it's a day, it's a DAY-O." The teacher would stop her piano to shush me with a finger pressed to her mouth while her eyes slowly widened, something that my mother did when she was angry and meant business.

I sang with gusto. Among a horseshoe of children who sat crosslegged on the floor, beaming good looks and washed faces, I sounded off with the conviction of a criminal. When we came to the end—the best part for me—I lowered my voice to a bass, bowed my head slightly, and raised my eyes as if to take a peek inside my frontal lobe.

I remember when our mothers came to open house at school. We kids, decked out in our best, sat on the floor in a horseshoe to sing "Red River Valley" to the mothers who stood with their coats on in the front of the class. The teacher blew into her harmonica for the right pitch and then hummed another pitch, which was the cue for us to hold hands. Some mothers touched their hearts.

I saw my mother look plain faced at me. I was happy, though. Mother's going to be proud. She's going to clap even before I'm finished. When we began I went along with the others, but toward the end I got carried away—"But remember the Red River Valley/and THE ONE WHO LOVES YOU SO TRUE!" The teacher, strumming her guitar, made her eyes big at me, and Mother, who was taking off her coat, mouthed silent words that meant trouble if I didn't knock it off.

After our presentation, the mothers viewed our art work that we kept in our cubby holes. Smiling almost demonically, Mother picked me up roughly from the floor, but became soft as we walked over to look at my art work that was kept in a folder that glittered with stuck-on stars that spelled my name. "Pretty, mi'jo," she said before she peeled open my scrapbook of people on fire, houses on fire, a dog whose furry face was black smoke. Page after page, she puzzled over my drawings, only to close it and walk over to the teacher who shrugged her shoulders and said, "Who knows?"

I was no good at drawing or singing, but I was pretty good at half-remembering. One morning our teacher, who always took off her bracelet, watch, and ring to fingerpaint with us in the morning, gave a scream at music time when she rested her hands on the piano keys. Her ring was not on her finger. She got up and frantically searched her desk, the tables, our lunch-boxes, before she turned to us—little kids on the floor—and asked if anyone of us had picked up her ring from her desk. The ring was pretty, she said, but it was naughty of us to take things without permission. None of us said a word. Some of the girls looked at the boys. I stared down at my shoes, which were new and black as cockroaches, and remembered playing with the ring at recess when all the kids were outside. But where was it now? I bit my lip, thought deeply, but failed to remember where I had left the ring.

When no one answered she lined us up to check our pockets, but stopped when the girls began to sob. Our teacher left the room sobbing, only to return, red-eyed and shaky, with our principal who shook a finger of threats at us, even when the girls and one sissy boy began to cry. But he couldn't pull it out of us—a diamond wedding ring. I looked down at my shoes, scared inside but stupid-faced and seemingly unworried.

They searched the rest of the morning—our pant pockets hung like tired tongues. They frisked our pant cuffs and stripped off our shoes, which they shook and tapped against their palms. Worry darkened the principal's face. He made us get on all fours to search the floor. We crawled on the floor—little girls were sobbing, tough boys were mooing like cows and having a great time.

Our teacher cried. The principal clicked his tongue in disgust. When school let out I played in the yard for a while and then walked home, supremely happy, with a fiery sailboat pinned to my shirt and singing "It's a day, it's a day, it's a DAY-O." And the ring? God knows.

Left Hand, Right Hand

I'VE STOLEN THINGS IN MY LIFE, BUT IT SEEMS I OWE SO
much more than I've taken. I first stole a toy car from the
Japanese kid on our block who had everything. The second
thing I stole was a box of maggots—or were they silkworms? To
this day, I don't know what they were, except that they were
white handfuls of movement in a box in the alley. I picked up
that box and carried it home, hiding it in the bushes. I squatted and made small penguinlike steps into the cavernous leaves
where I stirred the box with a stick as I tried to figure out what
the movement was. Bugs? Baby chickens? Spider eggs? They
were the size of fingernails, white and smelly. They moved as if
they were trying to say something. This scared me. But I didn't
leave or look away. I studied their motion until the smell overwhelmed me and I had to scramble out of the bush and into
the house. I washed my hands and face, but the smell stayed.
That night I closed my eyes, and the white movement stayed.
The next day I returned to the bush and, with a quick peek
inside, carried the box back to the alley. I hurried home to
wash my hands and face and listen to the radio to keep from
thinking of what the white things were possibly saying.

After this adventure I was good for a month or so, but
returned to taking things, like my mother's lipstick, which I
placed in the street to see a truck smash it into a paste, and my
brother's St. Christopher, which I tossed into our plum tree
and forgot about, until only last week. Then I stole combs,
earrings, and matches from the top of my parents' chest of
drawers. I gave away my sister's shoes and let the dog have her
sweater. I stole my cousin's Popsicle from the freezer but
denied it, even though a yellow stain smeared my face like

laughter. I was slowly becoming evil, but made a spiritual U-turn when I became a Catholic in the first grade. Once again I had become good and, consequently, guilty about my past. I repented, feared God. I made a resolution to stay away from my five-year-old sister, who went around on a sassy blue bicycle and cussed up a storm.

I was constantly tested. I saw fruit hanging from my neighbor's trees, red as sin. I fingered the loose change in the dish my mother kept in the cupboard. I held back playground punches and talked with girls about our Dick-and-Jane readers. Every Sunday I went to church, hands pressed together in prayer and head lowered. I looked at my shoes, occupied with the shine that I was sure everyone had noticed when I first walked in.

I remember one day when I was especially tested: it was a ritual for kids around our block to get together at a mom-and-pop store near our grammar school. There we bought penny candies: Tootsie Rolls, Abba Zabbas, jaw breakers, licorice that wagged from our mouths like donkey tails. That day I didn't have a penny. I went in but stood back watching the other kids argue and shout what candies they were going to buy. I watched them, enviously. Roy was rolling jaw breakers between his palms, waiting to pay. My brother was slapping a strip of black licorice against his wrist. I watched them until I could no longer stand it and squeezed between two other kids, placing my left hand on a Tootsie Roll and my right hand on a cinnamon sucker. Shame overwhelmed me, but I thought of the sweet bite that would roll in my mouth all the way to first grade. My hands started to close slowly over the candies, then opened suddenly. They started closing again, only to open more suddenly. My hands lay quiet on them, taking a rest. Then they closed again and this time stayed closed. But I couldn't move my hands away. They stayed on the candy rack, two quiet crabs, as my mind said Yes No Yes

No. Finally it was a Yes and my hands pulled away from the rack. To my amazement the grocer, who had been watching me, said, "Two cents!" I looked up, scared. I didn't know what to do. I opened up my hands and there they were, two candies. I looked up to the grocer who was looking down at me, mean as a dog. I placed them on the counter. I told him that I also wanted to get a light bulb.

"What kind?" he asked, bluntly.

"A little one," I said, pressing my thumb and index finger together and squinting at the air between them.

He showed me a shelf where the bulbs sat between sponges and dish soap. I said they were all too big and he pushed me to the counter where he showed me a tray of flashlight bulbs. I measured the bulbs between my fingers. Too small, too big, funny shape. None would do. I bunched my face with lines as best I could, and worried out loud because I needed that bulb real bad. He made a sour face. He slid the tray back under the glass case and told me to get the hell out of his store. And I did. I ran to school, with shame like a red stain of candy on my face.

Animals All Around

FOR MY CHILDHOOD FRIEND JACKIE AND ME, THERE WAS
no recognition of animal life, other than cats and dogs and an
occasional squirrel that from a distance looked like a baseball
mitt nailed to a tree. We lived on a broken block in a city that
could come to an end only if you owned a car. You could drive
to the foothills, and beyond to the Sierras, or to the crashing
sea inspired by calendars given away by banks each December.

We had cars but went nowhere, for our stepfathers were
beaten with work that made little money. On Saturdays they
sat in front of the TV—robots of flesh with unblinking eyes—
or mowed the lawn and set sprinklers that blossomed water in
all directions. They gulped beers and thought of water: the sea
with just enough wind, an umbrella, a spread blanket, and an
ice chest of sandwiches and beers.

On Saturdays, knowing that we were not going anywhere,
even though the television said we should go places—Beav and
his family in white clothes on a picnic and Fred MacMurray
tapping his pipe on a redwood tree at Bear Mountain—Jackie
and I got together in an alley behind my house to climb trees
and believe we were somewhere special, Yellowstone or the
Grand Canyon.

What do you see, I would ask, and he'd push me and speak
in a whisper: bear, deer, beaver thing. I looked where he
pointed, gawking like a fool, and shot whatever it was dead.
They were put to good use: flogged into hamburgers, skinned
and shaped into furry coats that dwarfed our small faces even
more.

Sometimes we went farther: Africa. Lions sunned on racks
and rhinos, muddy as shoes, stood knee-deep in grass. We

shot them with our fingers shaped into pistols. But they only blinked. It took an arm, stiffened into a bazooka, to open their eyes and send them running.

But we didn't go to Africa often. We stayed in America with our own animals. We stayed in the trees, Saturday after Saturday until, finally bored with it all, we climbed down from the trees and begged and cried to go places where animals might be. Our fathers told us to get the hell out of the house and our mothers, subtler but just as tough, made their eyes big with anger and threatened to make us rake leaves or weed a flower bed—the hard labor of childhood. We ran out of the house, scared of work and the meanness behind their eyes that threatened to activate their spanking hands.

When this happened Jackie and I took off on our bikes to Roeding Park. We stood at a pond, frothy green with algae and dotted with milk cartons. With a stick we tapped the cartons to the edge, only to throw them back when two black kids, in T-shirts that ended at the belly buttons, warned us to leave them alone. We threw them back, scared but ready to run them over with our bikes if they gave us trouble. But they didn't. They asked if we were brothers. I told them I was Mexican and Jackie was Okie. We passed questions back and forth, and then rode off to the zoo, stopping first to climb the Sherman tank, a monument to WWI behind a chain fence spray painted gold, and then to scan the horizon of picnickers chugging sodas in the afternoon sun.

At the zoo, we locked our bikes to a parking meter and hurried to the entrance where we tried to walk in without being noticed. But we were pulled aside, almost roughly.

"It's a dime," a man in a blue coat said.

We walked away without the usual routine of patting our pant pockets or blaming each other for the lost dime. We hurried around the corner out of view of the gate keeper, thinking of what to do. We stopped in our tracks when we heard the elephant trumpet. Jackie looked at me, and I at him with an exaggerated excitement. We punched each other in the arms and raced around the zoo, looking for an excluded place that would allow us to climb the fence. We found one near the garbage bins. On our knees we pressed our faces to the chain links. We saw leaves and smelled a rudeness that puckered our faces. Still, we started climbing, our fingers gripping the fence hard as we scaled upward. At the top we rested and scanned the trees for monkeys that might drop on us. We saddled the barbed wire carefully, our crotches almost nicking the wire. I swung my leg over, frightened as I ever was and even more frightened when I spotted an ostrich strutting in our direction.

"Look," I said to Jackie. He looked where I was pointing. He crossed his eyes at the ostrich, then lost his footing, so that his body stuttered down the fence, with a rope of blood following. He got up, stunned by the fall, and crying because blood was bubbling from his wrist.

An animal keeper, with buckets in his hands, hurried over yelling why in the hell was he fooling with the ostrich. He peeled Jackie's hand from the wound, and blood flecked his shirt like a fountain pen gone haywire. He backed away with a "Goddamn kid." He pulled a handkerchief from his pocket and again peeled Jackie's hand away to tie the slash closed. He looked up at me. "And what you doing up there?" Fear caught in my throat. I almost started crying but wised up. "I saw this kid fall," I said, "I wanted to help—swear to God!"

But he wasn't listening. He turned to Jackie and pushed him in the direction of a gate that would lead to the emergency room and maybe the cops who could come to get me. I climbed down, raced to my bicycle, and rode back to the Sherman tank where, on top, I waited for Jackie to come out with a white bandage, big as a flag, tied to his arm. I waited an hour and when he didn't come out I rode home with a chicken bone of fear poking my throat. At home I tried to be good. I went outside and began pulling weeds from the flower bed. I raked the alley. I took out the garbage. At dinner I used my napkin fourteen times and ate slowly as I made conversation. Then it came: the phone call from Jackie's mother. I sat in the bathroom. I heard my mother say, "Oh these kids, if it's not one thing it's another."

Then she hung up. A moment of silence passed. I heard her sneak to her bedroom and search the closet: a thin belt doubled in her hands? She walked on tiptoes to the bathroom, then pushed hard, thinking that she would catch me off guard. No such luck. I stood behind a locked door, begging.

"Mommie, listen," I cried, "Jackie did it, not me. He wanted to see the elephants, and I told him not to do it." I could sense her eyes burning holes into the door. Fear crawled my back like a fidgety fly. She rattled the door, yelled, sweettalked me with a mouthful of Juicy Fruit gum. She slapped the door with the belt and pounded for me to open up. But I refused. I remained in the bathroom shivering and praying for a way out other than the door. Then I made my move. I pulled open the door and dashed for the living room, thinking all the while that someone—brother or irate mother—would pounce on me. But no one stopped me, except myself. I peeked out the front window. Mother was on the front lawn talking with my Aunt Frances. I stepped onto the porch, quietly closing the screen door behind. When my aunt wriggled hello with her fingers, my mother, whose back was to me, turned to look over her shoulder.

"I'll take care of you later," she said and went on talking with my aunt. I carried my limp soul to the alley, climbed into a tree, and searched the places where Jackie and I saw animals, big animals that could take care of the world and save a kid's life against all mothers.

Oranges and the Christmas Dog

FOR CHILDREN, CHRISTMAS IS THE ARRIVAL OF GIFTS, AND, at age ten in sloppy clothes and misshapen clown's shoes, I wanted my share. I was greedy for something, anything, even the oranges and pens my stepfather's mother pressed into our arms. We knew those simple gifts that Pearl brought us were at least worth unwrapping, worth smiling and crowing, "Nice pens! And thanks, Pearl, these oranges are really, really good!" I could have hopped the fence and gotten free oranges from our neighbors. But I figured why make a face about an expected gift, especially since my stepfather—drunk in his recliner, his head hovering over a TV tray stamped with dead presidents—would have bellowed about our ungratefulness.

Children expect gifts, and if Baby Jesus shows up, that's fine, too. As a Catholic, as a fourth grader at St. John's Elementary School, as a worrier for the poor and the children of Biafra, I wanted Baby Jesus to be born, wrapped up, sung to, adored, celebrated . . . all that. But then I wanted him—and I'm sorry to say this—pushed aside so that I could get *my* presents. That year I ruined all the expectation of Christmas by tearing tiny holes in the wrapping of my three presents. With the roving eye of a surgeon examining the insides of stomach guts, I peeked at what the bright wrapping hid: one was a jigsaw puzzle, another a sweater, and the third a rifle. Even with my limited view, I could see that the rifle didn't cock like the more expensive toy rifles, the kind the rich kids would get. Mine was just a length of hard plastic with which to point at my neighbor Johnny or my little brother Jimmy or even my own head and sputter, "TUTUTUTUTUTU. You're dead!"

I peeked at my presents while my older brother was outside

trying to kill time until Christmas, two days away, a slow drip of minutes like a leaky faucet. He had to do something to keep his mind off the presents.

"I know what I got," I told Rick as I walked toward him on the frost-hard front lawn. With the fog shrouding Fresno, the neighborhood of ancient houses was dead. Only kids or really dumb people would venture out into that chilling scene. Maybe we were both.

"You peeked, huh?" he said. He was eating free oranges from the neighbor's house. "You stupid!" He knew that I had wrecked my happiness. Now I would have to wait an entire year, until next Christmas, before that overwhelming yearning for presents would possess me again. A strangeness filled me.

"I got a rifle," I mumbled.

"I picked it out," Rick said.

"You're lying," I said.

"It's a green rifle," he said, the final slice of his orange going into his mouth.

Then I thought that maybe this mean brother of mine had picked it out, and, in fact, picked out a cheap one so that Mom could buy him better presents. I felt angry as a ferret, my breath shaping up into a fist in front of my face. But before I could put my anger into action, the neighbor's dog, who was shamefully underfed, walked over. His fur was like a dirty carpet on an overturned chair. Without a collar or the tinny chime of dog tags, this canine of mixed breed appeared naked. His ribs clearly showed.

"Watch this," Rick said. He pulled an orange from his jacket and clawed it roughly, juice dripping from his fingers. He took a slice and fed it to the dog.

"He likes 'em," Rick said.

The dog closed his mouth around the orange slice, let it rest there for a moment. Then his furry chin began to churn, a trail of juice leaking from his mouth.

Poor dog, I told myself, he's really hungry. I took the orange from Rick and dug my fingers into that tropical fruit, then held out a piece. He took a step on the frosty lawn, and I began to think *his paws are cold without any shoes.* Once I had walked barefoot from the house to the car to get a comic book. Those thirty or so steps hurt, and I couldn't imagine having to walk on frost all winter, only to pad about on hot asphalt when summer arrived.

Rick left, leaving me with the dog, who raised his watery eyes to mine, and something like a groan issued from the cave of his lungs.

"Don't go away," I told the mutt. I dashed into the house and threw open the refrigerator, for wasn't a starving dog an immediate emergency? I pulled open the meat drawer and eyed the baloney, the precious lunchmeat for my stepfather, a warehouseman. I carefully peeled off a single slice, set it on a piece of bread, and covered it with a second piece. But in my hand, the sandwich lacked the weight that might fill in a starving dog's ribs. Again I scanned the meat drawer: a chunk of hard yellow cheese. I broke that cheese into crumbs and sprinkled it onto the sandwich. I considered spanking this concoction with mayonnaise, reconsidered, and hurried outside.

"Hey," I called on the front lawn. The dog had walked part way up the street. He turned his head slowly around, then his body, and sat down, feet together. I hurried to him.

"You need to eat," I told him. I shoved the sandwich at his mouth, and his nose, black as oil but dry as a leaf, sucked in the smells. He sniffed, then took a small bite. I figured that he was so hungry, so tired, that he could eat it slowly, one little bite at a time.

"You're going to be okay," I told him, my hand rifling through his fur. He finished the sandwich and I went back inside for milk. What was better than milk to wash down a sandwich? It took a while to find something to use, something other than a cereal bowl, which would bring on the Mom's wrath if she found out I was feeding a dog from our dishes. I returned with a soup can brimming with milk. I had to walk slowly, one careful step at a time, the frost crunching like bones under my shoes.

"Where are you?" I called to the dog, who had moved like a shadow further down the street. Once again he turned his head, and followed with his body. He sat down in front of Mrs. Prince's house.

"You like milk, don't you?" I asked as I got closer.

The dog didn't reply with a bark. He didn't appear any friskier from the sandwich or relieved that someone in his life-time was concerned. I thought that maybe he would see me as a sort of savior, for wasn't it Christmas, or nearly Christmas, a time of rebirth? But his eyes leaked water, his sadness as ancient as the flow of the Nile.

"Here," I said, poking the can under his nose. He sniffed its contents before slowly lapping it until his snout was nearly drowned in milk. I poured milk, splash by splash, into my palm and let this new friend quench his winter thirst.

"That's good, huh," I said.

The dog turned away, done with me, fed but maybe unsat-isfied, his lifeless tail like a shoestring. I placed the can on the curb intending to pick it up later. But I heard a tap-tap on a window: Mrs. Prince had parted her front window curtain and shook a finger at me. I waved and picked up the can. I chased after the dog, who plodded more like a *burro*, with a slow and almost clip-clop action of hooves.

We stopped at the corner of Angus and Thomas. The streets were dead in the cold, metal-gray afternoon. The sun would not reach us that day.

"Where do you want to go?" I asked.

The dog looked straight ahead. Then, like a zombie, he

crossed the street. I followed, probing, "Where are you going? Huh? You're going to get lost!"

I remembered from somewhere—a nature program like "Wild Kingdom"?—that a sick elephant left the herd when it knew it was dying. I was scared. Was this dog pacing out the distance from our block to where he would finally roll on his side, kick his paws into the air, and die.

"You ain't sick, are you?" I asked.

I stopped him by hugging him around his neck, which was warm as blankets. I looked him straight in the eye, my own face appearing on the surface of his watery eyeballs. That scared me even more, that I was suddenly part of this dog's life, a picture on the windows of his vision. I knew that animals didn't have souls, or so the nuns taught me, but I could see, however briefly, that my presence held meaning for this dog. His tail began to wag.

I rubbed his back, building up the friction of heat. I patted him and ran my hand over his head, slendering his eyes, two more teary drops leaking away with the picture of my face.

"Let's go back home," I told the dog. If I had been meaner, I would have cursed the owners of this dog, a family of renters who had shown up one day. They lived two houses from us, and we were told to stay away from them, three sickly kids whose bodies were broomsticks. My mother thought they might have TB.

"Come on," I begged the dog. "Let's go back. I got another sandwich for you."

I turned him around and pushed and prodded, beckoning him to return to our block, which had nearly disappeared in the fog. Our block, I thought, was like an altogether different town, with different people with different cars and jobs and, if the doors were flung open, a whole set of kids I didn't know. The block was unfamiliar.

I walked alongside the dog, whose pace had quickened, as if

he was in a hurry. Had he been human, he might have looked at the watch on his wrist. He started to run, not fast but fast enough that I threw the soup can to the curb and broke into a jog. I had deeper worries than littering.

"You're going to get lost!"

The dog cut erratically across lawns and into the street, heedless of the occasional cars with their sinister headlights frisking the leaf-strewn street. He slowed for a moment, then trotted up someone's lawn and onto the porch. I didn't dare climb the steps of the porch; my mom always warned us to stay out of other people's yards, advice I usually ignored on my block. But here, in this strange place, I stood on the sidewalk. I was cold. My nose was red and I was jumping from foot to foot.

"Come on," I whispered to the dog, who sat on the porch. He sat only a brief moment and then climbed down the steps and made his way to the back yard. He acted as if he belonged there, the family pet instead of a stray.

"No! Don't go over there!" I yelled.

The dog didn't look back. I thought he was on his way to his grave, the place to lie down in fog. And when the fog cleared, he would be gone. I stood on the sidewalk, not sure what to do. The giant sycamore dripped water on me. The cold worked into my bones. I rubbed my hands together, gathering up heat, waiting for the time he would eventually reappear from the back yard. As I stood there, I recalled how in second grade I had asked my mom if there was a chance that one day I might become a saint. I had just returned home from St. John's Elementary and I wanted more than anything to be holy by feeling for the poor, who were so plentiful. I don't remember her answer.

I figured here was my chance to approach sainthood, my chance to walk alongside the dog until it was time for him die. I must have waited on the curb, freezing, for two hours. I eventually ventured into this back yard, whispering, "Come on, boy. Come on!"

I raised my eyes to the windows. Any moment a large man would come out yelling for me to go away. He would have a gun or a stick to whack sense into me. That's when I discovered that not only was the dog gone, but I was no saint because I was ready to give up so soon. I felt ashamed, then mad. When I returned home, the dog was back on his porch. He had cut through that yard, leaving me standing in the cold.

"You're *bad*," I scolded the dog, who didn't even seem to recognize me. He sat among orange peels and ripped-up newspaper. One of the broomstick kids came out. His skin was nearly transparent, and his eyes were sunken.

"Leave my dog alone," the kid said.

I did. I returned home, stiff from the cold, and after, I stood over the floor furnace, wandered into the kitchen. It was four thirty, dark outside. A few orange-colored porch lights came on, cutting through the fog. The dark descended on us. Soon Mom was home from work, followed by our stepfather, who took his place in his recliner, the TV on and coloring the walls. We ate dinner and then Pearl showed up with gifts of pens and oranges. It was two days away from Christmas, but we were allowed to open one present each. Pearl looked on, face heavily rouged, smiling and hoping that we would pick hers. And we did, my brother and me. I tore into that poorly wrapped present. I smiled up at her, for wasn't it Christmas, a time to be appreciative, like a dog? I dug my fingernails into the oranges, a mist and scent atomizing that moment when I knew that I was no saint. I tore into my orange and fit not one but five slices into my mouth. I chewed, churned the juicy pulp, and swallowed for Pearl, such a happy woman, who waited for me to clear my throat and say once again, "Thanks, Pearl, these oranges are really, really good."

TWO

Like Mexicans

MY GRANDMOTHER GAVE ME BAD ADVICE AND GOOD ADVICE
when I was in my early teens. For the bad advice, she said
that I should become a barber because they made good
money and listened to the radio all day. "Honey, they don't
work como burros," she would say every time I visited her.
She made the sound of donkeys braying. "Like that, honey!"
For the good advice, she said that I should marry a Mexican
girl. "No Okies, hijo"—she would say—"Look my son. He
marry one and they fight everyday about I don't know what
and I don't know what." For her, everyone who wasn't
Mexican, black, or Asian were Okies. The French were
Okies, the Italians in suits were Okies. When I asked about
Jews, whom I had read about, she asked for a picture. I rode
home on my bicycle and returned with a calendar depicting
the important races of the world. "Pues sí, son Okies tam-
bién!" she said, nodding her head. She waved the calendar
away and we went to the living room where she lectured me
on the virtues of the Mexican girl: first, she could cook and,
second, she acted like a woman, not a man, in her husband's home. She said she would tell me about a third when
I got a little older.

I asked my mother about it—becoming a barber and marrying Mexican. She was in the kitchen. Steam curled from a
pot of boiling beans, the radio was on, looking as squat as a
loaf of bread. "Well, if you want to be a barber—they say they
make good money." She slapped a round steak with a knife,
her glasses slipping down with each strike. She stopped and
looked up. "If you find a good Mexican girl, marry her of
course." She returned to slapping the meat and I went to the

backyard where my brother and David King were sitting on the lawn feeling the inside of their cheeks.

"This is what girls feel like," my brother said, rubbing the inside of his cheek. David put three fingers inside of his mouth and scratched. I ignored them and climbed the back fence to see my best friend, Scott, a second-generation Okie. I called him, and his mother pointed to the side of the house where his bedroom was a small aluminum trailer, the kind you gawk at when they're flipped over on the freeway, wheels spinning in the air. I went around to find Scott pitching horseshoes.

I picked up a set of rusty ones and joined him. While we played, we talked about school and friends and record albums. The horseshoes scuffed up dirt, sometimes ringing the iron that threw out a meager shadow like a sundial. After three argued-over games, we pulled two oranges apiece from his tree and started down the alley still talking school and friends and record albums. We pulled more oranges from the alley and talked about who we would marry. "No offense, Scott," I said with an orange slice in my mouth, "but I would never marry an Okie." We walked in step, almost touching, with a sled of shadows dragging behind us. "No offense, Gary," Scott said, "but I would *never* marry a Mexican." I looked at him: a fang of orange slice showed from his munching mouth. I didn't think anything of it. He had his girl and I had mine. But our seventh-grade vision was the same: to marry, get jobs, buy cars and maybe a house if we had money left over.

We talked about our future lives until, to our surprise, we were on the downtown mall, two miles from home. We bought a bag of popcorn at Penney's and sat on a bench near the fountain watching Mexican and Okie girls pass. "That one's mine." I pointed with my chin when a girl with eyebrows arched into black rainbows ambled by. "She's cute," Scott said about a girl with yellow hair and a mouthful of gum. We dreamed aloud, our chins busy pointing out girls. We agreed that we couldn't wait to become men and lift them onto our laps.

But the woman I married was not Mexican but Japanese. It was a surprise to me. For years, I went about wide-eyed in my search for the brown girl in a white dress at a dance. I searched the playground at the baseball diamond. When the girls raced for grounders, their hair bounced like something that couldn't be caught. When they sat together in the lunchroom, heads pressed together, I knew they were talking about us Mexican guys. I saw them and dreamed them. I threw my face into my pillow, making up sentences that were good as in the movies.

But when I was twenty, I fell in love with this other girl who worried my mother, who had my grandmother asking once again to see the calendar of the Important Races of the World. I told her I had thrown it away years before. I took a much-glanced-at snapshot from my wallet. We looked at it together, in silence. Then grandma reclined in her chair, lit a cigarette, and said, "Es pretty." She blew and asked with all her worry pushed up to her forehead: "Chinese?"

I was in love and there was no looking back. She was the one. I told my mother who was slapping hamburger into patties. "Well, sure if you want to marry her," she said. But the more I talked, the more concerned she became. Later I began to worry. Was it all a mistake? "Marry a Mexican girl," I heard my mother say in my mind. I heard it at breakfast. I heard it over math problems, between Western Civilization and cultural geography. But then one afternoon while I was hitch-hiking home from school, it struck me like a baseball in the back: my mother wanted me to marry someone of my own social class—a poor girl. I considered my fiancee, Carolyn, and she didn't look poor, though I knew she came from a family of farm workers and pull-yourself-up-by-your-bootstraps ranchers. I asked my brother, who was marrying Mexican poor that fall, if I should marry a poor girl. He screamed "Yeah" above his terrible guitar playing in his bedroom. I considered my sister who had married Mexican. Cousins were dating Mexican. Uncles were remarrying poor women. I asked Scott, who was still my best friend, and he said, "She's too good for you, so you better not."

I worried about it until Carolyn took me home to meet her parents. We drove in her Plymouth until the houses gave way to farms and ranches and finally her house fifty feet from the highway. When we pulled into the drive, I panicked and begged Carolyn to make a U-turn and go back so we could talk about it over a soda. She pinched my cheek, calling me a "silly boy." I felt better, though, when I got out of the car and saw the house: the chipped paint, a cracked window, boards for a walk to the back door. There were rusting cars near the barn. A tractor with a net of spiderwebs under a mulberry. A field. A bale of barbed wire like children's scribbling leaning against an empty chicken coop. Carolyn took my hand and pulled me to my future mother-in-law who was coming out to greet us.

We had lunch: sandwiches, potato chips, and iced tea. Carolyn and her mother talked mostly about neighbors and the congregation at the Japanese Methodist Church in West Fresno. Her father, who was in khaki work clothes, excused himself with a wave that was almost a salute and went outside. I heard a truck start, a dog bark, and then the truck rattle away.

Carolyn's mother offered another sandwich, but I declined with a shake of my head and a smile. I looked around when I could, when I was not saying over and over that I was a college student, hinting that I could take care of her daughter. I shifted my chair. I saw newspapers piled in corners, dusty cereal boxes and vinegar bottles in corners. The wallpaper was bubbled from rain that had come in from a bad roof. Dust.

Dust lay on lamp shades and window sills. These people are just like Mexicans, I thought. Poor people.

Carolyn's mother asked me through Carolyn if I would like a *sushi*. A plate of black and white things were held in front of me. I took one, wide-eyed, and turned it over like a foreign coin. I was biting into one when I saw a kitten crawl up the window screen over the sink. I chewed and the kitten opened its mouth of terror as she crawled higher, wanting in to paw the leftovers from our plates. I looked at Carolyn, who said that the cat was just showing off. I looked up in time to see it fall. It crawled up, then fell again.

We talked for an hour and had apple pie and coffee, slowly. Finally, we got up with Carolyn taking my hand. Slightly embarrassed, I tried to pull away but her grip held me. I let her have her way as she led me down the hallway with her mother right behind me. When I opened the door, I was startled by a kitten clinging to the screen door, its mouth screaming "cat food, dog biscuits, *sushi*. . . . " I opened the door and the kitten, still holding on, whined in the language of hungry animals. When I got into Carolyn's car, I looked back: the cat was still clinging. I asked Carolyn if it was possibly hungry, but she said the cat was being silly. She started the car, waved to her mother, and bounced us over the rain-poked drive, patting my thigh for being her lover baby. Carolyn waved again. I looked back, waving, then gawking at a window screen where there were now three kittens clawing and screaming to get in. Like Mexicans, I thought. I remembered the Molinas and how the cats clung to their screens—cats they shot down with squirt guns. On the highway, I felt happy, pleased by it all. I patted Carolyn's thigh. Her people were like Mexicans, only different.

First Love

To know you're in love you have to step outside, walk up the street, and be so alone, so flogged by your separation, that your mind will race your heart and almost win. I did this one fall when I was twenty and so dazed by the separation from my girlfriend, who was on vacation, that I thumbed her photo in my room, confessing my one lust for another woman. Guilt caught like a chicken bone in my throat. I paced the room. I looked out the window. Yellow grass. Scraggly vines. Noisy sparrows in trees that were so thin that nothing could hide behind them.

I was rooming with my brother and two artist friends: one painted monkeys reading books in different places—subways and over-stuffed chairs—and the other shaped and pressed clay into elephant feet which he sold as ashtrays. My brother, an artist also, airbrushed eggs and red balls in the blue of untraveled space. In other words, the household was crazy. I couldn't turn to any one of them, open a beer, and spill out my story. Instead I put on my coat, went downstairs, and, looking left, looking right, went back upstairs to drag down my bicycle. I started off slowly in high gear, but to keep from thinking of Carolyn, I rode faster. I passed City College and busy intersections into the residential streets with names like Poplar and Pine. Leaves shattered beneath my wheel and I loved the sound. I rode slowly admiring the lawns, the children puffed up in down jackets, and the feathery smoke of chimneys. The October sun was behind an overcast sky, almost breaking through, almost making shadows where there was only gray.

I stopped at a pharmacy in the Tower District and read

magazines until the cashier, a woman with blue hair, adjusted her glasses so often that I finally got the message. I bought a candy and, to keep from thinking of Carolyn, I immediately picked up my bike and rode so fast that things looked blurry and confused my eyes. I pedaled in the direction of the canal where I and Benny Jeung, a friend of many years, had ridden inner tubes through languid days of our best summers. I stopped my bike. I stood at the water's edge to look down at the dark water of leaves and sticks. I sat on the weedy bank tossing rocks, and thought of Carolyn and what she might be doing in Canada on her vacation. It must be like here, I thought. Lots of leaves. Cold sky. Few people going about. I blew out a puff of white breath, and thought she might be doing the same by some river, quick with salmon. I saw her in a sleeping bag, the lantern at her side throwing out an aura of heat and light. She was writing postcards, one after another. She brushed back her hair that kept falling into her eyes as she hurried little messages to her family and her new lover, me. Growing sad, I got up and started off again because I didn't want to think about her. I rode to the Fresno Mall where I bought a bag of popcorn at Woolworth's, and walked up and down the aisles that glittered with toys, pans . . . and record albums at half-price. From there I went to Gottschalks where I dreamed of new clothes, bright Kensington shirts and stiff Levi's.

I rode to South Fresno, the place of my birth, and in an abandoned house on Sarah Street searched closets where I found overcoats, vests, and shoes seeming to sleep on their sides. On the back porch sat a stack of newspapers, musty stories from the fifties. What a find, I glowed, and carried an armful back to the apartment where, with my roommates who put down their brushes, I sat on the floor reading about deaths and weddings and housing tracts going up not far from where we lived. The four of us said very little as we bit our lips and read with knitted brows while the newspapers made a dull rustle in our hands when we turned the pages, fanning a musty smell into the air.

But after a while my roommates got up, one by one, and went back to their art. I sat alone with a pile of newspapers, with their stories and ads and brown photographs of women in dresses like frilly lampshades. When the cat nudged my leg, I thought of Carolyn who was probably reading a newspaper in Canada. She was in the lobby of her hotel, leg wagging as she waited for her friend to come back from making a telephone call in the bar. Again growing sad, I folded the newspapers and put them out onto the balcony. When I came back in, when I couldn't think of anything to do, I gave up and went to my bedroom to indulge, to hover over the photograph of my girl-friend standing by a tree, smiling. Beautiful, I smiled back. I looked out the window and things were beginning to disappear in the dusk.

All day I had tried to keep my mind from thinking of her, this first love. Ride a bicycle. Pick up things, put things down. Talk with my brother, with my roommates. Feed the cat four-teen times. Now I was alone, willing to surrender myself to a deep longing. To do it right, to think of the woman who mat-tered in my life, I put on my jacket and went downstairs again, but instead of taking my bicycle I walked up the street that got longer with each step. The farther I got from my apartment, the clearer the picture of her became, so that after a few blocks I was talking, almost singing, as if she were right next to me, her feet moving a little quicker to my longer strides, but keep-ing up so that we could be together for that walk and others.

Secrets

IT'S DIFFICULT TELLING SECRETS, ESPECIALLY IF YOU'RE
married as I've been for nine years. Last night while my wife
stepped from the bathroom, pink from a shower, I sat in bed
thumbing through a magazine and thinking about what I've
not told my wife, from would-be lovers to my small fears, like
waking up to find spiders staring at me from inside my shoes.
     My wife stood before the mirror, her skin slowly cooling
under a nightgown, and worked face cream into the little lines
around her eyes that will someday mesh into other lines. I
watched this nightly ritual: she dabbed into a jar, made circular motions with two fingers from her brow to her throat, and
dabbed again. She plucked at her eyebrows and studied her
face as if she were meeting someone new. Finally she came to
bed. We read together: a novel for her and a magazine for me.
I adjusted my pillow, fixed another on top, and cocked my
elbow so that my head rested in my palm. But after a while my
neck hurt, so I lay on my stomach with my magazine in front
of me. But I couldn't concentrate on the words or even skim
the cartoons and the ads that announced shiny things I
needed. I rolled onto my back, eyes on the ceiling. My mouth
slowly curled into a smile when I thought of a secret I could
tell my wife, a secret that would not hurt but only amaze. I
wanted to make her put down her book, screw up her face,
and think, "Who did I marry?"
     I wanted to roll onto my stomach and, with a squeezing
hand to her hip, snuggle my face into her neck and say,
"Honey, let me tell you a story." I rolled onto my side but
didn't say anything. I smiled. She turned her face to me, smiling. An hour later we were asleep.

I have a friend whose father enjoyed a secret for twenty years. He is a big rancher who talks loudly, who slaps his thighs at Henny Youngman jokes, drinks two beers at once, and talks about the money he keeps in his cellar (gold bars next to homemade jams) to anyone who will listen. But he is also a man who can keep quiet, saying few words when everyone else is stalking up a storm. He let go of his secret one slow Saturday when he said to his family, "Let's go for a drive." His wife ignored him and kept piling rinsed dishes into a rack. His children went outside to climb into trees. But the father packed a bag of fruit—oranges and apples—and took down blankets from the hall closet. In a few minutes his family was shooed into the car, their faces pressed to the windows as they sped down a road that was new to them. An hour later they were at a small rural airstrip. He pointed to a yellow plane. The children raced to be first, ducking their heads as they climbed into the back. The children jumped up and down. The wife was scared, then mad, as she demanded that he stop acting like a fool. He slapped his thighs, started the engine, and gunned the plane down the runway until it lifted with a bounce that had everyone screaming to get out. The sky went blue; the trees seemed no bigger than puddles. The plane climbed toward their town of Exeter, and buzzed their house to the wife's embarrassment because the neighbors had come out to gawk.

His secret was that he could fly a plane. The secret I wanted to share with my wife was that I had once rented an apartment in San Francisco. Better yet, I shared an apartment with a woman who had recently come back from a four-year stay in Greece. It was a harmless arrangement. She had a bedroom and I had my own, though often we shared lunches: soups and avocado-and-tomato sandwiches at a small kitchen table where we talked softly as lovers. But we weren't. I was married and she was engaged to a Bulgarian living in Greece. We bit into sandwiches, slurped soup, and talked about the secrets we kept from our better halves.

With a thermos of coffee, we sometimes sat in rickety chairs on the roof, five flights above the noise of traffic. The days were bright. The Golden Gate stood like a harp in the distance and the bay seemed bluer than we could remember. Sailboats moved slowly, or not at all. Smoke rose from freighters. Glare smeared the windows of the apartment buildings on Nob Hill. Now and then a couple from another roof would look at us and we would look back until they turned away, pointing to something of interest in the not-so far distance.

I stayed there for a month to find out what it would be like to spend my days in San Francisco. My wife didn't suspect where I went. It was summer, school was out, and my wife thought I spent my mornings reading in the Berkeley Public Library and the afternoons playing racketball in Golden Gate Park. But I wanted to tell my wife about it, to turn to her in bed, brush back her hair, and kiss her neck for a little noise before I began telling her what I had done two summers before. I wanted to tell her while we were in bed, with books and magazines. "Carolyn," I would begin, "sometimes do you think I'm a little crazy?" She would nod her head yes at her novel. She would smile at the pages and then lift her bright face, eyes like shiny triangles. If I told her, I would have to hold her in my arms and begin slowly with sailboats and freighters and the bay seen from a roof top before I placed an innocent but married man in an apartment with a worldly but single woman. Then she would catch on and her hug would turn into a squeeze that would hurt. Squeeze, squeeze, and the whole story would come out like toothpaste. A little crying, a little laughter. "You're a crazy one," she would say and during the coming nights, if not weeks, she would hug me and ask for more secrets. "Please, sweetheart," she would coo. If I said there was none, she would squeeze until I had to make up something with sailboats and freighters, and a man and a woman who looked out to a body of water that was bluer than what they remembered.

Money

SOMETIMES IT'S MONEY THAT I WANT. I OPEN MY PASSBOOK and see the numbers rise and fall from $2,300 to $850 to $1,200. The figures are black as rain that won't let up. Black, and more black. I'm amazed where it goes—the big chunks I mean—because when I look around the room there's nothing I can remember buying. The couch has been here for years, first as a cow and now as a place for my daughter to jump up and down . . . until she pops over the edge, head first and already crying. The table has been here for years. The chairs. The refrigerator. The bed was given to us for having a baby, and the dresser that's followed us from place to place like a good dog is cluttered with things that seem foreign: a hat, dolls, a basket of spools, and a school of black whales the size of thumbnails.

I look out my window: my car is a 1966 Chevy, blue as a piece of sky. The lawn is old, the trees, the walk pushed up by a stubborn root trying to make its way under the earth. On the side of the house, though, the hedge is gone. I remember spending money there. I hired a friend to pull it out, a burly black guy who, during lunchbreak, ate sandwiches and chips and played my guitar on the steps, to the amazement of an older couple who were holding down their hats as they walked to church.

I paid him one hundred and twenty dollars to rip out the hedge. I paid him forty dollars to haul pieces of concrete. He lugged them like typewriters, grunting when he threw them onto the bed of his truck. Another thirty went to hauling weeds. Another thirty went to pruning a tree that's now bare as a hatrack and perhaps just as fruitless. We'll just have to see in spring.

But that was not much money. Where had the rest gone? I know there's rent and groceries. Our daughter is now in school. Dresses smother her closet; books are staggered against the wall like ancient ruins. But she demands very little—literally. Little saucers, little skirts, and little shoes. A big day for her is a handful of sand in a park or toy cars overturning in the grass. And there are her friends, girls with scuffed knees and running noses. But they are almost free, except for chocolates that invariably stain their dresses.

Maybe my wife is spending the money. She does have clothes with names I can't pronounce. Her shoes look like they're standing on tip toes—high heels the color of lipstick. She has a fur coat but she's worn it for years, even before our marriage. It's a thrift-shop coat with a rip in the armpit, so when our daughter and I point at airplanes or statues or bridges lit with cars, she just stands there with hands in her pockets, smiling but not joining in on the fun.

My wife hasn't made up her mind who she wants to be. She seems to be spending money. A line of perfumes, like foreign soldiers, stands on the dresser. She taps a fragrance on her wrist and the back of her knee, and asks, "Guess who wears this kind?" When she opens up her drawer, scarves pop up like magic. When she opens one of her many lacquered boxes, cheap jewelry that's really expensive glows like crying eyes. There are, of course, the make-ups that blush and highlight and cover what should be seen. One day she looks girlish with the no-make-up look; another day she is the hard, MBA Asian, with eyebrows like hatchets.

I admit I spend money. I admit that I buy lunches (even when my wife packs me a lunch of a sandwich and an apple) at restaurants that serve food from countries that are barely on the map, like Ceylon and Liechtenstein. And I admit that I sometimes buy clothes I don't need—jackets and sports coats, shirts and Italian slacks with designer labels that can't be seen without getting intimate. The other day I was foolish, but not foolish enough to make myself look good. Alone, without my wife and her eyebrows raised into hatchets, I test drove a BMW through Oakland and into Piedmont, past two-story homes with feathery smoke rising from chimneys. At a quiet corner I idled the car, a smirk starting up in my soul, and then raced the car so that the leaves in the street seemed to fly. But in the end, I said I'd talk to my wife, shook the hand of the salesman who wouldn't let go even as I walked backwards, and got back into my Chevy for the drive home and a Sunday dinner.

Today it's money that I want, a deep green in my wallet when it yawns open at clothing stores. "Cash, sir?" asks the salesman whose own wallet is toothless, a piece of leather with no bite.

"Yes, this will be cash," I say and peel twenties into his out-stretched hand. At a restaurant, when the check comes on a black tray, I pull out a wallet that growls for me to open up. I pay and pay some more when I go outside to buy flowers that do tricks to my eyes.

But who knows why I feel this way. Perhaps it is a stage in my life when money is happiness. I find this difficult to believe, though, because last week I said to my wife that we should be poor, really poor. If we looked out our front window, we would see hard dirt; if we looked around the living room, we would see lint scuttling like clouds across the floor. "It's really a rich life—being poor, honey," I said. She said "umm, ummm" into the mirror as she plucked her eyebrows into even fiercer hatchets, a towel wrapped into a turban around her washed hair and body still steaming from a jungly shower. I talked and talked as I dressed. My wife walked around my words and me as she prepared for dinner and a movie and, later in bed, said in a breathy voice, "What do you want more than anything in the world?" "I want you, right now"—I replied. "It's going to cost you, silly boy," and she squeezed me for all that counts.

Finding a Wife

IT'S EASY TO FIND A WIFE, I TOLD MY STUDENTS. PICK ANY-body, I said, and they chuckled and fidgeted in their chairs. I laughed a delayed laugh, feeling hearty and foolish as a pup among these young men who were in my house to talk poetry and books. We talked, occasionally making sense, and drank cup after cup of coffee until we were so wired we had to stand up and walk around the block to shake out our nerves.

When they left I tired to write a letter, grade papers, and finally nap on the couch. My mind kept turning to how simple it is to find a wife; that we can easily say after a brief two- or three-week courtship, "I want to marry you."

When I was twenty, in college and living on a street that was a row of broken apartment buildings, my brother and I returned to our apartment from a game of racketball to sit in the living room and argue whether we should buy a quart of beer. We were college poor, living off the cheap blessings of rice, raisins, and eggs that I took from our mom's refrigerator when Rick called her into the backyard about a missing sock from his laundry—a ploy from the start.

"Rick, I only got a dollar," I told him. He slapped his thigh and told me to wake up. It was almost the end of the month. And he was right. In two days our paychecks from Zack's Car Wash would burn like good report cards in our pockets. So I gave in. I took the fifteen cents—a dime and five pennies—he had plucked from the ashtray of loose change in his bedroom, and went downstairs, across the street and the two blocks to Scott's Liquor. While I was returning home, swinging the quart of beer like a lantern, I saw the Japanese woman who was my neighbor, cracking walnuts on her front porch. I walked slowly so that she looked up, smiling. I smiled, said hello, and continued walking to the rhythm of her hammer rising and falling.

In the apartment I opened the beer and raised it like a chalice before we measured it in glasses, each of us suspicious that the other would get more. I rattled sunflower seeds onto a plate, and we pinched fingersful, the beer in our hands cutting loose a curtain of bubbles. We were at a party with no music, no host, no girls. Our cat, Mensa, dawdled in, blinking from the dull smoke of a sleepy afternoon. She looked at us, and we looked at her. Rick flicked a seed at her and said, "That's what we need—a woman!"

I didn't say anything. I closed my eyes, legs shot out in a V from the couch, and thought of that girl on the porch, the rise and fall of her hammer, and the walnuts cracking open like hearts.

I got up and peeked from our two-story window that looked out onto a lawn and her apartment. No one. A wicker chair, potted plants, and a pile of old newspapers. I looked until she came out with a broom to clean up the shells. "Ah, my little witch," I thought, and raced my heart downstairs, but stopped short of her house because I didn't know what to say or do. I stayed behind the hedge that separated our yards and listened to her broom swish across the porch, then start up the walk to the curb. It was then that I started to walk casually from behind the hedge and, when she looked at me with a quick grin, I said a hearty hello and walked past her without stopping to talk. I made my way to the end of the block where I stood behind another hedge, feeling foolish. I should have said something. "Do you like walnuts," I could have said, or maybe, "Nice day to sweep, isn't it?"—anything that would have my mouth going.

I waited behind that hedge, troubled by my indecision. I started back up the street and found her bending over a potted geranium, a jar of cloudy water in her hand. Lucky guy, I thought, to be fed by her.

I smiled as I passed, and she smiled back. I returned to the apartment and my bedroom where I stared at my homework and occasionally looked out the window to see if she was busy on the porch. But she wasn't there. Only the wicker chair, the plants, the pile of newspapers.

The days passed, white as clouds. I passed her house so often that we began to talk, sit together on the porch, and eventually snack on sandwiches that were thick as Bibles, with tumblers of milk to wash down her baked sweet bread flecked with tiny crushed walnuts.

After the first time I ate at her house, I hurried to the apartment to brag about my lunch to my brother who was in the kitchen sprinkling raisins on his rice. Sandwiches, I screamed, milk, cold cuts, chocolate ice cream! I spoke about her cupboards, creaking like ships weighed down with a cargo of rich food, and about her, that woman who came up to my shoulder. I was in love and didn't know where to go from there.

As the weeks passed, still white as clouds, we saw more of each other. Then it happened. On another Saturday, after browsing at a thrift shop among gooseneck lamps and couches as jolly as fat men, we went to the west side of Fresno for Mexican food—menudo for me and burritos for her, with two beers clunked down on our table. When we finished eating and were ready to go, I wiped my mouth and plucked the sole five-dollar bill from my wallet as I walked to the cashier. It was all the big money I had. I paid and left the restaurant as if it were nothing, as if I spent such money every day. But inside I was thinking, "What am I going to do?"

Scared as I was, I took Carolyn's hand into mine as we walked to the car. I released it to open the door for her. We drove and drove, past thrift shops she longed to browse through, but I didn't want to stop because I was scared I would want to hold her hand again. After turning corners aimlessly, I drove back to her house where we sat together on the front porch, not touching. I was shivering, almost noticeably. But after a while, I did take her hand into mine and that space between us closed. We held hands, little tents opening and closing, and soon I nuzzled my face into her neck to find a place to kiss.

I married this one Carolyn Oda, a woman I found cracking walnuts on an afternoon. It was a chance meeting: I was walking past when she looked up to smile. It could have been somebody else, a girl drying persimmons on a line, or one hosing down her car, and I might have married another and been unhappy. But it was Carolyn, daughter of hard workers, whom I found cracking walnuts. She stirred them into dough that she shaped into loaves, baked in the oven, and set before me so that my mouth would keep talking in its search of the words to make me stay.

Colors

IF NOT AN APPLE IN ONE HAND AND DESIRE IN ANOTHER, IF not a novel and characters falling in and out of love, then something of that Saturday morning when you and I drove to Reedley, your hometown, where we walked its main street, hip to hip, my arm around your shoulder, your arm around my waist. We window-shopped, pointing at gleaming sale items. The 20% off toaster, the 30% off blender with ten speeds, the freight-damaged luggage at half off. We sat on a bench in a small park and watched sparrows, twig-brown, fly away with twigs and grass; one even flew away with a cotton ball. We wandered through a drug-store and stopped at the magazine rack. *Glamour* was a month old, dusty when you picked it up and thumbed a breeze in our faces, stopping at a page that was mostly words, not ads for clothes and perfumes and Cinderella shoes. You looked up and said, "My favorite color is red, red and black." I smiled the shallow smile of happiness, not paying attention to what you had just said, or why. Then I thought about it, and was baffled. It didn't follow or make sense. Why did you all of a sudden acquaint me with your favorite colors? Later, however, when I was back at my apartment and on my bed, exhausted from trying to keep up my end of the conversation, it would sink in as a truth: you were starting to tell me about yourself, little by little. First colors, then later movies and books and old boyfriends, one who was married and wouldn't leave you alone. The magazine in your hand was a thing to hold as you talked.

I had done the same. Outside on the street I mentioned that my favorite color was forest green and, your hand tightening around my waist, you asked, "What color is that?" I tried to describe it by saying that it was a color like a large forest seen close up. That didn't seem clear. I said it was like a tree with moss or maybe just the moss itself, and said that it was one of the colors in the 64 Crayola box. We left Main Street and walked aimlessly through the residential streets, where a dirty dog poked his wet nose around your knees and tried to go higher. I told you how when I was in the third grade Sister Marie made the class break their crayons in halves. She said that we could color better that way, and that Van Gogh, Monet, and Whistler worked with crumbs and sliver-thin pastels. We could do the same, Sister Marie reasoned, and make pretty art like the masters. Some of the girls cried as they broke their crayons, and I didn't feel great about it either because it was my first 64 Crayola.

We had walked from town to the river where we stared at the water, its surface full of autumn clouds and the branches of the cottonwoods. I became quiet and transfixed by the movement of the river. My brother came to my mind, how he used to rock-jump at Piedra to see who would fall first. I laughed to myself and told you that I was thinking of my brother. You didn't say anything. You watched my eyes, which were so young that they didn't know what to settle on, you or the water and the image of my brother inside my head. I talked about Rick, poor artist, and about myself and how when I was young I thought of becoming an oceanographer but now knew I was lousy at math and wasn't math something you needed to study the sea? I talked nonsense until I ran out. When you leaned against me, I took two steps back and leaned against the rock. I brought you into my arms, kissed, moved my hands up and around. I took your hand and led you into some brush where we kissed more, lay on wet grass, and marveled at the sky that was faraway yet right before us. I shivered, and then you shivered when I told you that stars were really ice. I wasn't sure. But it sounded right. We then got up, your hand in mine. I took a leaf from your hair, two tangled in your sweater, but put them back when I lay with you again.

Going Back

My wife and I are devoted to Masterpiece Theatre, which is about the only television we watch, except for the best boxing matches and an occasional football game. We look forward to Sunday, nine o'clock, and the television throwing out its blue light and a good story; we look forward to hurrying Mariko to bed where she'll read for fifteen minutes before my wife and she say a pagan-style goodnight chant:

> Sotooda Odooda
> Podewda codewda
> AHOOH Permew
> Peacock Penguin
> Pegasus Unicorn Butterfly
> Stubby, the best and only goat we know.

Sunday night offers a little silence, a little solitude, a time away from our daughter. And like so many other parents, we enjoy an hour to ourselves, an hour in which the telephone is unplugged, the child is asleep, the half-written letters are put aside, and the demands of the house are unanswered—the sagging roof, the wood rot in the windows, the mystery of the water heater that snaps and rumbles when the toilet is flushed.

We crawl into bed, pillows propped up behind us, with one lamp making shadows that seem exciting. Then Alistair Cooke appears, cross-legged and elegant, one hand touching his brilliant, silver-streaked hair as he wets his lips and says, "Good evening. Tonight we're in the fourth episode that takes us . . . " And we're off, witnessing Claudius' stutter, Poldark's manly dismount from a horse, Lilly's glitter from champagne and jewels like tears on her breast.

It's not wholly the drama that keeps us sitting before the television, Sunday after Sunday, as it is the ritual of my wife and me being together, almost touching, almost tender, even with our hands that are greasy from popcorn. Now and then I will look at her, and she will squint her eyes, lovingly. Now and then she will rub my thigh and I'll move it closer until I'm almost sitting in her lap. It's a happy hour that is seldom long enough.

The second time I held my wife's hand was at the movie *Sounder*, on March 19, 1973. I remember that date because I wrote it so many times in my notebook that I can't forget it.

That night at the movie my hand crawled like a dizzy crab into her hand, which she snapped up to my surprise. I looked at the screen for two hours, oblivious to what was going on. I couldn't throw my heart out to the characters of a story that didn't make any sense. Love-struck, my heart made noises under my shirt and sweater. I held her hand without looking at her, though occasionally I stole a quick glance at her hand that was over mine.

Later, I put my arm around her shoulder as we walked to the car and, still later, at my apartment, I snuggled my face into her neck and kissed and kissed until she was saying, "No, Gary, please no, which meant, according to my older brother, "Yes, yes, please!" I stopped, however, and offered Carolyn a bowl of ice cream, which she ate heartily. To keep her there longer, I offered another bowl, but she declined. Placing the bowl on the coffee table, she shivered from the cold, a perfect cue for me, and I leaned against her, my face again meeting hers. I said soft words; I brushed her hair from her eyes and outlined her brow with a finger. I played with a button, then another, until she was again saying, "No, Gary, please no," which of course meant yes to about everything.

So it still goes, thirteen years later. It began in a theater and continues on Sunday nights with Masterpiece Theatre. That is, it continues if we can get Mariko to sleep, a child who is very good but already a ferocious reader who likes to stay up. A month ago we let her read in bed for half an hour before we turned the lights out. Thinking she was asleep, I sneaked into the kitchen to make popcorn and lemonade. When I started back to the bedroom with two tumblers pinched in one hand and a bowl in the other, I heard Mariko call from her bedroom, "What are you doing?"

Caught like a rat, I looked at her in the semi-dark, "Mom and Dad are going to watch their program." I looked at her and she at me, knowing that that wasn't what she wanted to hear. I glanced down at the lemonade and popcorn. "And we're going to have a little snack."

At first she didn't say anything but only looked at me with mournful eyes. Then she said, "Sounds like you're going to have a wonderful time."

"Lie down, pumpkin," I said lamely. I opened our bedroom door and Carolyn, who had already turned on the television, beamed a smile as I entered. I put down the tumblers and bowl on the side of the bed and knelt to tell Carolyn what Mariko had said.

"Oh, poor baby," she said sadly. "She's such a good girl."

"Let me get her," I suggested. I got up and carried her back as if she were flying, arms out like Wonder Woman's. She crashed into the pillow, utterly happy to be with us, to sit between us tossing popcorn into her mouth, big as a moon.

June

LAST NIGHT I DREAMED ABOUT JUNE BARRETT, A GIRL from my high school. I dreamed that we were again side by side as we raced for A's in history. I felt her presence without looking at her. She was sitting with her back straight, hands quiet as flowers on her desk top, and legs pressed together as if she were holding a quarter between her knees. But she didn't need that coin. She could have opened up her legs and let it drop, rolling wildly until it flopped on its side, exhausted. Later, after class was dismissed, I could have picked up that quarter, bought a Coke, and dreamed about her with my eyes wide open.

She came from a good home in Sunnyside. A pool gleamed and rubbed light in her backyard, while a row of feathery trees bounced in the wind, casting shadows that made the grass seem even greener. Her mother was a mother in fine dress, not a fat terror with a folded belt. She stood over an electric range, stirring dishes I couldn't pronounce. "Filet mignon," she would say, "Consommé, capers, cornichons." When her family sat down to dinner, candles shone in their eyes. Their talk was soft. The music was soft. The food in their mouths was noiseless. They chewed, not chomped; they swallowed, not gulped; and they asked for bread, not jumped with grabbing hands for the bigger pieces.

So it was June, the good daughter. June walking among autumn leaves with her best friend, June doing homework or talking with her father who could talk, not mumble with the TV on. June sleeping with a half-smile. June reading *Seventeen* while her childhood Teddy looked on from a high shelf, his eyes shiny as wet rocks.

Last night June Barrett came back in my sleep. She asked

for me, said words, and almost touched my sleeve. She raised her hand when the teacher scanned the classroom. Answered Virginia 1808. Answered California 1949. Her hand shot up again, and again, and again. That was all. Some flashes in my sleep, light being thrown together to shape her face, the class-room, those years—and she was gone.

But I want to go back to high school and tell her things of my heart; how I walked through those days, thinking of her dresses, shoes, and lunches. I remember the happiness of her hair that bounced when she walked. She smiled the perfect teeth of magazines, the ones I scribbled black in my mean-ness, my bitterness, because her smile would get it all—the shiny cars, the houses, the beachfront vacations where she would sip tropical drinks with a lover or husband in the late haze of afternoon. The boy who cleaned up would be some-one like me: brown, quiet, and so thin he would be hardly noticed among the chairs.

June, the bright girl, the college-bound mind among lesser minds—those who would become janitors, warehouse-men, and car salesmen in mismatched shirts, pants, and loud jackets. I was among the lessers she never saw. I wanted to talk with her, to sit near a splashy fountain and tell her about my life or say something almost important. Look at this about me, I would say. And look at this, and this.

The one time June noticed me was when my friend Scott and I waited in front of the school for his mother to pick us up. We leaned against the chain-link fence, doing nothing among the nobodies when, to our surprise, then to our embarrassment, his mother drove up in a truck the color of a pumpkin. A banged truck. An Okie truck coughing blue smoke. She called us above the engine noise. She jerked her thumb over her shoulder, gesturing for us to hop in the back. The cab was stuffed with tools, canvas tarps, jacks, and tangled rope. What were we to do? We were punk kids with tattoos

penned on our wrists and motor oil stinking up our hair. We
jumped into the back and at first felt foolish as the truck
coughed around the school, parading us for what we were
worth. I tried to crouch low but there was no place to hide,
unless I lay like the dead, face up and looking at the sky. But
the bed was puddled with oil and stinky as a shoe. So I squatted. I listened to Scott laugh ignobly. I laughed with my hair
full of wind, laughed and thought, Who cares?

Maybe June Barrett cared. At the corner I saw her in a station wagon, and she saw me before I had a chance to turn my
face away. She smiled like a friend. I smiled back as the truck
lurched forward so that I had to grip the side or fall over like
a bowling pin. That smile of hers stayed with me at the next
intersection, and every other intersection for the next three
years. I couldn't get it out of my mind—that smile that was
more a reflex than a greeting.

From Scott's place I went home without hanging around to
fool with his car, which was up on blocks in his backyard. I
closed my bedroom door and listened to the radio for a song
whose words I could steal and offer to June. But none came,
fuzzy from the speaker. I got up, went to the backyard to kick a
ball against the fence, and jumped that fence to walk the alley,
first in silence and then quietly talking what troubled my heart.

June Barrett, June Flores, June Oda. They enter our lives
like bright shadows and pass us up as they make their move for
the good jobs and even better lives. They slip into business
suits the color of money, and hurry up steps, their hair
bouncing from eagerness. They talk and make sense. Drinks
are passed around from a serving tray, and their smiles,
reflexes like springs, open up.

I dreamed about June Barrett last night. Her hands lay on
her dress and her legs were pressed together. I saw this. And I
saw her raise a hand for the teacher to call upon her. Even in
dreams, she knew the answer.

Blue

How much sky do we need? If we're going to remain whole, healthy in mind, we need to walk, dream, lie inquisitively under the sky each day, or so writes a researcher who thinks neurosis arises from our disconnection from the sky. Look at the major cities—say New York or San Francisco—where the sky is often eclipsed by buildings, crossed up with wires, slivered and cut into pieces by bridges and towers, so that we can never look up to an unbroken sky. We get portions, flimsy postcards of blue, from where we sit at work or slouch at home. In such cities neurosis is prevalent, more visible daily than in places where the sky is not blocked out but fills the day and rains its complete, unfractured blue. Arizona. Montana. Canada. Those are the places. Australia. Africa. I only half-remember the places and don't recall how the researcher came to study this phenomenon, but I believed him.

When I was a kid of ten or so, a time when I could wander as I pleased, the sky seemed to show up more often, especially when my friend Jackie and I sat in fruit trees: orange, apricot, plum, and peach. We walked up alleys until we found one heavy with fruit half-guarded behind a wire fence and leaped so carelessly that sometimes we fell and got up with dust powdered on our eyelashes. We climbed trees and ate like birds, pecking holes in fruit that we dropped unfinished to the ground. We liked plums the best—the juice splashed against the insides of our cheeks and the roofs of our mouths. It excited us. When we smiled, our teeth were red and dripping.

After eating our fill we stayed in the trees to talk. And about what? Girls we were in love with, God, family, mean brothers on bicycles, school fights that did no one any good. As we spoke we seldom looked at one another. Instead, we looked skyward where, if it was spring, an occasional cloud chugged by, sloshing a belly full of rain, and if it was summer, the blue was the color of a crayon. I remember that well. I also remember Jackie and the beatings his father gave him, his body balled up under a bed and screaming *Daddy No!* I said these things too, and almost cried. Because we confided in one another with our eyes on the sky, we felt less troubled when we finally did drop to the ground and went back to our homes where, however slowly, it would begin again.

I remember the Fresno sky after a rain and how puddles flashed like knives when I walked past on my way to nowhere in particular, just looking about as I walked from my street into an alley, happy that I was outside and things were as clear as they were going to get in my young life. I walked toward Jackie's house, but instead of calling him I sneaked into his backyard, tore a couple of pomegranates from his tree, and raced down the alley to another friend's house. When I called and no one came out, I climbed onto his pigeon coop and up onto the roof of his garage. There I tore open a pomegranate whose juice ran like fingers of blood down my sleeve to my elbows. While I ate I looked around until the sky seemed more beautiful than I remembered: the clouds were piled up, like fat Chinese faces and, from where I sat, the Sierras in the east were tipped white with snow and jagged like a child's scribbling. It was the first time I had seen them, snow or no snow, with so much blue behind them.

That was when I was ten. Now that I am so much older, the possibility of climbing a tree to eat fruit with a friend is almost nonexistent. How would I explain myself if someone, neighbor or wife, looked up among the ladders of leafy branches and saw a pant leg, a shirt, and finally a face, which would be mine. And what friends would climb for fruit they could enjoy on the ground?

But it's not a tree you need or a friend. It's the sky and the feeling that you're connected, that things are circular, beginning with the sky and all it holds: sun, moon, stars, wind, birds that come and go with the seasons.

I believe this more and more. Lying on a blanket at Tilden Park, I have listened to the wind in the trees recalling a childhood day, a friend, my wife, my daughter with clever tricks up her sleeve. I've lain half in shade, half in sun, and recalled all that I've enjoyed and, on occasion, have tried to clear my mind so that the sky is my only thought, its brightness like no other. When I close my eyes, the blue stays. When I listen to the wind, the blue stays. And a little green that makes me think of the sea.

Waiting

ONE DAY IN THE SUMMER THAT MY FATHER WAS TO DIE, A bird flew into our house where it banged into walls and curtained windows. Its noisy beating scared my sister so that she ran to her bedroom until the bird was gone. We needed a broom, a dish towel, and Father's loud hisses to drive it away. It left by a window, perching outside on a wire, quickly shifting its black head in different directions. By the time I ran outside to throw a rock, it was on the neighbor's fence. The bird swooped away into a far tree, out of range. A month later, in August, Father was dead from an accident at work.

This past July a bird found its way inside my sister's apartment. A window? An open door? We don't know. My sister had come home from shopping to find the bird on the dining table, its black stare like the one she saw years ago. Debra put down her groceries, careful not to disturb the bird, and opened the sliding glass door, the front door and windows. With a dish towel spread like a net, she slowly approached the bird that stared at her with an open beak. When she waved the towel, it flew and banged into the wall, letting loose feathers that slowly drifted downward. It flew again when she threw the dish towel and missed. Eventually the bird found its way to the porch where it stood profile so that one eye blinked at Debra. It blinked, jumped onto a rail, and was gone.

It was a death sign. Either someone was going to die, or the dead were present in the house, perhaps standing by the floor lamp or next to the chair where Debra sits to read the evening paper. The dead could press up to her face in sleep, and she wouldn't know. The creak from the bed could be the dead; the flash from the bathroom mirror could be the someone from the past. For the next few days she was careful. Work, people, and quiet intersections loomed in her mind as threats. She guarded her sons, not allowing them to go outside alone—or if they did, she watched from the window as they rode their bikes or played ball. She stood by, knowing that they might slip and fall and not get up.

And a week later, a robin flew into my house. I woke to a sound of things falling from shelves, and when I got up from bed a robin was at the front window looking out. It jumped, fluttered at the glass, and came down. It jumped again and flew into the bookshelves, dropping like a gray fruit to the floor.

I stood back, my heart racing, and I was so awake that my hair was lit with fear as the robin beat against the walls and windows. I opened the front door and went to the kitchen for a broom. When I came back I couldn't do anything. I sat on the couch watching the robin watch me as it strutted along the window, its claws clicking with each step. Finally I poked with the broom, so that the robin beat its wings and left by the window.

It was early morning—little after six—and a gray bank of clouds was pressed against the Berkeley hills. I went outside to try to follow the robin's flight, that crossed over the neighbor's house and out of view. I went back inside. Not knowing what to do, I returned to bed where I lay thinking of my wife and daughter and how the dead were in the house. I knew this. I closed my eyes and thought my father had come back to say something. He was here, or someone else was—a dead uncle in his tattered clothes. I listened to the house creak and the water heater fire up. When the morning newspaper popped against the porch, I flinched. I got up, dressed loosely in jeans and T-shirt, and went to the next room to see my daughter whose face was flushed pink from sleep. I went outside to the backyard to the study where my wife sleeps when she sews late at night. I rocked her hip to wake her, but stopped to hurry back inside when I thought that Mariko was alone. When I returned through the front door, the robin was standing in the fireplace looking at me. A chill ran like a zipper up my back. It flew awkwardly and banged the ceiling, and I hurried to get the broom.

The robin left by a window and didn't come back; for days afterwards I stayed home, venturing only to the backyard to watch Mariko play in a sand pile. I was careful in my movements. I picked fruit from the apricot tree only if I could reach them from the ground. I stayed away from work—hammers, shovels, ladders.

I listened to the house for signs. The creak of wood. Night breathings. The knock at the door and no one standing there when you opened. My sister came over the next evening. With my wife we sat at the kitchen table where we talked until we stopped to quiet our fear. I told her to be careful, not to do anything. These birds were either a death sign, the dead themselves, or maybe a curse (earlier in the summer, before Debra had moved to Berkeley from Fresno, she woke up one morning to find raw meat on her front steps. Pink meat on white butcher paper. A sign, our mother said, someone wants to hurt you).

Now these birds. Something is happening, I thought. I remembered that my father had died when I was five; my daughter was five that summer—my daughter who is so much like me in face and manner. And I'm like my father, in face and manner. I told my wife about these feelings, and she was scared, so troubled that she couldn't sleep that night, and the next day she refused to let me go outside. I stayed in bed reading and listening for the house to tell me things. My daughter came often, with the *shish-shish* of her slippers, to read stories that ended in a happy life.

I waited all summer for that bird to come back and show itself as my father, gone so many years. I waited for him. I listened to the curtains move and the floor tick. Sometimes the sunlight on the floor—and even that cat who scratched a small hole in the yard and left it open—had meaning. I watched my daughter whose palm was mine, whose face was mine. I refused to let her go into the yard alone because he was there, just waiting.

"Don't come now," I said to Father all summer. Those days were so gray that he could have been anywhere.

White Blossoms

LAST DECEMBER I DROVE TO DOWNTOWN SAN FRANCISCO to look for a gift for my wife, and no matter where I turned— left or right, up and down difficult hills—I couldn't find parking. The streets were clotted. Shoppers hugging awkward gifts in their arms jaywalked as they pleased without looking. Finally I nudged my car into a tight space six blocks from it all—I. Magnin, Macy's, Neiman-Marcus—and was walking with hands in my pockets and my jacket collar raised like a sail against the city wind when I saw three girls—third graders, I imagined—waiting at a crosswalk for the green light. Leather bags were strapped to their backs, and they were dressed in red plaid skirts, white blouses, and green sweaters—Catholic girls on the way from school?

Then I saw others, in twos and threes, and a stray one on a knee tying her shoe. I saw an uneven line of boys running after them and then still another group of girls. The boys caught up but stayed behind, almost in step but talking and laughing loudly.

These children brightened the gray day and the gray adult lives they walked among. I hurried after them because I was surprised to see them—school children in the middle of traffic, shoppers, and tall buildings. I caught up with them but couldn't find the words to ask my simple question. I didn't want to scare them, to make them stop and ask why I was asking. They would have looked up at a stranger with windblown hair and dark skin, and would have turned away, hoping that I would leave.

I wanted to talk with them. I wanted to ask about their school and about themselves. Do you like The City? Where are our brothers and sisters? Which bus do you take home? A few days before I jogged on the track at Berkeley High and afterwards I sat, then lay with eyes closed, on the grass. Two girls about fifteen talked nearby, first giddy about a boy in their class, and then serious about their divorced parents whose lives were loose ends of old arguments. I listened and caught myself listening. This surprised me. I never thought I was so curious about others, especially teenagers with semi-punk hair. But I was. I caught most of their words and worried about their lives, even after the girls were gone.

I walked behind the children slowly, stopping now and then to peek into store windows—propped-up best sellers, winter clothes draped over chairs and ladders, kitchen knives hanging like threats by fishing line from the ceiling—so that I wouldn't overtake them. I walked quietly. I heard the girls spell "elephant," "rhinoceros," and "bureau." A spelling contest among themselves? A rehearsal for tomorrow's quiz? A girl in braids used her fingers to spell. With each letter, a finger sprung up like a fat, stiff worm, and went down again when it was needed for another letter.

I left them to their spelling and childhood laughter, and walked toward Macy's, still curious about them because they were so small, little kids in the rush of noise they call The City. The buildings, gray as a slate sea, dwarfed them and made them look fragile; the urgent taxis forced them to step back on the curbs and almost hold hands. The children were braving the elements and smiling through it all.

In the lingerie department at Macy's, I ran my hands over robes. I took one that I liked off the rack, twirled it on its hanger so that it flared open like a flower, and then checked the size, the price, and the tab that said it was washable. I asked the saleslady about the color.

"White," she said, rubbing the cuff between her thumb and index finger. "This is just adorable!"

I stared squinting at the robe, and then looked at the saleslady. "No, no—I mean, is it a special white? Like 'eggshell white' or 'apartment white'?"

The saleslady said it was regular white, and not wanting to risk another question, I bought it. And I bought a pair of slippers that the saleslady said, in an assuring voice, was also regular white.

With these gifts under my arm, I left Macy's and walked up O'Farrell Street in the direction of my car but in no hurry because I knew I still had time on the meter.

Again I saw Catholic students—not the earlier ones but others. They were walking in twos and threes, and almost huddled together like small-time conspirators. Again I had the urge to ask them where they were from, what school. I was amazed by their presence because it seemed so unlikely that a school would be pressed between the tall buildings of downtown San Francisco. I was more amazed that these children could maneuver among pushy crowds with such charge, with such confidence. The way they laughed openly and argued over this and that, it seemed natural to sidestep the poor man with his beaten cup and the streets burst open by jack hammers. They walked past the woman in a fur and the wag of a tight dress, and the men with money on their minds. They walked past it all, bright and talkative and natural as kids in the suburbs.

I wanted to talk to them, but I knew I couldn't because I wasn't their father, uncle, or older brother with a good job or generous wallet. I let them pass, my curiosity still itching like a palm, but thought of them as I walked back to the car, envying them because they went to school in a city I would have loved as a kid.

But where was the school? I walked and walked, and asked merchants in small shops if they knew the school. They shrugged their shoulders, sucked on cigars, and let smoke issue from their lips. Some pointed gruffly toward Sutter. Others said they thought it was on Montgomery. I trudged up hills, around construction barriers, and even peeked into an alley, only to give up and return to a ticketed car.

Sometimes you never find out. White blossoms fall at your feet, and you can only guess where they came from, what bright wind blew them your way. They sputter in the air, lingering against the blue, and then are gone.

This Man (1)

MY FATHER DIED IN AN ACCIDENT, AND IT WAS NO ACCIDENT that the man who fell on him and broke my father's neck never again came to our house, though he was a friend of the family who lived only five houses away. He was that person who walked past our house every day on his way to Charlie's Grocery for meat, a head of lettuce, milk for his children. After our father's death he took a different route; he chose instead Sarah Street to get to the grocery.

I wonder how it was for him, what he felt. Nearly thirty years later I can see him in my mind. He's on the couch, tired from the work of candling eggs for Safeway, his boots off and shirt open; or it's summer, hot, and he's in the back yard staring transfixed at the water running from a hose into the garden. I see his wife shout from the kitchen that she needs butter. He gets up slowly and laces up his boots; he turns away from the river of water, already drying between the rows of squash and tomato plants, and coils the hose. He takes the quarter from his wife and, starting off to the store, thinks of Manuel, our father, maybe sees his face whole, maybe sees his face twisted and on the ground, the blood already drying like the water in the garden. But how much? How much of our father was on his mind? Did the kids in the street distract him, the neighbors on porches, a barking dog? Did he sing inside his head, worry about bills, maybe think of work and the eggs that traveled endlessly on the conveyor? He bought his butter, went home to eat with his children, who after the accident never came over to play with us. We waved to them when we walked past their yard and, behind their fence, they waved back.

Shortly after the accident we moved away from our south Fresno neighborhood, and he and his family became those names we never said in our house. Something happened in our family without us being aware, a quiet between mother and children settled on us like dust. We went to school, ate, watched television that wasn't funny, and because mother never said anything, father, too, became that name we never said in our house. His grave was something we saw in photographs; his remembrance those clothes hanging in the back of the closet.

I remembered this man from the old street when I saw him years later buying cigarettes at a gas station. I was filling the tires on my bike. His car was large, and he himself was large, his girth like a tree: I like to think he was eating for two, himself and father, who was inside like a worm taking his share; that after all those years he still thought of Manuel and the afternoon when he climbed that ladder with a tray of nails on his shoulder, lost his balance, and fell. This is my hope, for my sake and this man's, because we should remember the dead, call them back in memory to feel their worth.

He must have felt guilt and shame, or otherwise he would have walked up our street to the grocery or said more than "Hi" to me at the gas station. But it's not guilt or shame that I want to feel for him but sadness, that a man like so many others is dead and the photographs we own do no good in assembling Father once again into flesh and bone. We lived poor years because he died. We suffered quietly and hurt even today. Shouldn't this mean something to him?

Sadness not guilt. I have felt both. As a kid I often thought about the sea, yearned for the sea, and imagined that where I lived was the wrong place; that being poor and Mexican was wrong. During those years I thought of the sea a lot, not of Father, and am ashamed of this. It's so strange to me now: I had maps of the sea, books, model ships I set proudly on doilies for visitors to notice. I had questions for teachers—How big was Atlantis? Did the Vikings really discover America? Are Eskimos Chinese who live in the cold? This went on for years, my fascination with the sea, and for years I never dared mention my father to my mother or my sister and brother. He was gone, and we were here, and the man who did this to us was nowhere to be found.

It would take a doctor to explain our loss, or a wise man to sit me down and quiet my nervous knee that I can't stop. It's strange; my brother has the same tic. When we meet for Thanksgiving, his knee, like mine, jumps up and down. It won't stop. When I ask, "What's wrong," he says, with his arms folded behind his head, "Nothing. Nothing at all."

My Nephew

My nephew. My sister's boy. He's four and some months, hair full of wind and trouble. The other day I caught him pinching handfuls of pennies from the ashtray in my bedroom.

"What are you up to?" I asked.

"Getting rich," he said. He smiled up at me, looked down with a mixture of fear and comedy rubbed into his face, and wiped a few sweaty pennies from his palm back into the ashtray. He walked away, back to my daughter's room—my daughter who was in her reading corner, hiding, I suspect, because she too had a few pennies pressed like dark stars to her palm.

His name is Diego, but he also goes by the name of Popeye. Some day he just may become a sailor, for already his body, with its small shadows of muscle, is squat as a suitcase. When he's shirtless and hangs from the trapeze in the backyard, the muscles in his arms show themselves like tiny, unripe apples as he does chin ups. He lets go, grins like he means business, and runs around in search of something to whack with his rolled-up newspaper sword. Then he comes back, breathing hard and bobbing like a clown, and opens his palm for a penny in payment for his little show.

But Diego can be quiet and even a pleasure. With Mariko he will cut pictures from magazines and paste them on construction paper. While they work in the bedroom, the only sounds that issue from them are busy scissors and simple requests: "Gimme the paste." If somebody peeked into the room, he might think they were dwarf monks restoring a medieval manuscript—inking gold leaf on the corners of pages brittle as dead insects. They are quiet, absorbed in play and out of my hair.

Diego is the kid who pours sand in my daughter's hair, looks around with his tiny grin as she starts up her machinery of tears, and pours again. I know him as the kid who falls and laughs but cries when his mother leaves for work, his mouth open as wide as a doughnut. I could saucer one into his mouth, and that would quiet him, make him chomp down on the sweetness of life.

He's a strong but small kid who one day may run track, dance or twist his way to fame on the parallel bars. I can see him doing any of those, or even boxing, for there's a clear vein of meanness in him that may make him enough money to keep him away from the pennies in my bedroom.

But that day is years away. For now, I'm trying to teach him the ABCs. Last night we sat at the dining table studying the first seven letters of the alphabet. With Diego in my lap I sang and hummed these letters over and over, thinking if he heard their names enough they would make sense. I sang, and then he sang. When I thought he was ready, I asked him to say the letters by himself, but he grew quiet as he had no idea of what to say. He scratched at the letter D, as if he wanted to get rid of it. I squeezed his hand gently and asked him what this letter was, pointing to the A.

"G," he said. I said, "No, an A."

A few seconds later I asked him again, and that time he said, "W." Again I corrected him and squeezed his hand away from half-hiding the alphabet. We moved to B, then C, then D, and with each letter he stabbed in the dark, guessing once that the D was the number four.

But we practiced, and some of it sank in, because by the end of our half-hour session he could say the first three letters of the alphabet. I was pleased with this start. I made myself a cup of coffee and bragged to my wife that I was going to make

Diego into a little scholar. She smiled and ushered the kids into the bedroom to put on their pajamas. I went to the living room where I put my feet up on the couch and listened to them in the bathroom brushing their teeth. My wife joined me, her head like a tired moon on my shoulder. I listened to Diego gargle water and heard Mariko say, "Lookit. I got it for my birthday." I knew she was referring to a fancy soap pressed into the shape of a rabbit.

"What dat?" Diego asked. "An alarm clock?"

I laughed, splashed coffee on my robe, and knocked my wife's head gently with a knuckle as she rolled her eyes back. Diego ran by the door, happy as you can get in this life, and, fingers like a gun, shot *bing, bing, bing.* In bed we lay with arms behind our heads as we blinked at the ceiling, wondering about this kid who was in bed in the dark whispering, "Uncle, uncle, I got a nose."

On Our Own

MY DAUGHTER AND I ARE FENDING FOR OURSELVES. Yesterday we went to Golden Gate Park where we visited the Steinhardt Aquarium. We looked at lizards and toads that looked at us from their backdrop of sand and dead limbs that were supposed to be trees. But the toads, peppered with green spots, refused to meet our happiness no matter how often we tapped our fingers on the glass and laughed at the flies crawling on their squat heads.

I carried Mariko in my arms when we walked over to the pond and its false waterfall, half-hidden behind flags of broad banana leaves, which were real. Alligators were there, glueyeyed and seemingly dead. The turtles among them were busy in the pond, though. They bicycled their feet, bobbed in the waves they made, and climbed steadily up difficult rocks. Mariko enjoyed this; I smiled and ushered her toward the dark hall of fish tanks, stopping at each one for a glance.

But we stayed to watch the penguins, new acquisitions, turn sweetly in our direction, as if to say, "Hello to you!" They waddled, they dove into the greenish water, they faced each other like friends at a cocktail party. Mariko turned to me, utterly charmed. I smiled some more, thinking how much I wanted to be home with a beer and the TV turned on to just about anything. But I checked my greed. I whispered in her ear that she was sweet like them, this four-year-old who later at home would waddle like a penguin and dive into the couch, making the sound of water splashing.

So it was. We looked at fish, or what looked like fish, and wandered in the nature room where deer and beavers and antelope stood glassy-eyed and stiff in their fur. After this we went outside. We ate lunch on a bench and watched sparrows, those hoods of the air, bicker over spilled popcorn. They bobbed, they jabbed at crumbs, they scratched at the ground and fluttered their gray wings for no reason at all. We ate our sandwiches and, when we had had enough, we saucered the uneaten bread. They pounced on it, making noises that made passersby turn to see what was happening.

From there we went to the racquetball courts behind the museum. The Saturday crowd was there: Ronnie, Eliot, Hiro, Carlos. They were shirtless on the bench, sweat like yellow mist on their faces, while someone, who was only a familiar name, was talking about a talent show he had seen in the Mission. He stopped, however, when he saw me coming. The crowd greeted me with a "Hey dude" and my daughter with a handshake.

Mariko stiffened and averted her eyes, looking down in shy posture. I picked her up, bounced her in my arms, and told these guys that she was my daughter. Unshaven and almost seedy, Carlos said, "Wait a minute," and searched his backpack for an orange. He pulled out beers, a bag of sunflower seeds, balled socks but no orange. He shrugged his shoulder and asked if I was ready to play. I said no. I told him that my wife was out of town, that I had to take care of my daughter. And anyway I hadn't brought my gear.

We talked for a while and then left them, these ragtag men who waved bye-bye until we were out of sight. At home we played in the sand pile in the backyard. By then Mariko's nose was running and her knit hat was stuck with leaves because she had fallen so many times.

We went inside. When I took off a shoe, sand hissed on the floor. I was careful with the next one, and careful when I tugged off her pants for there was no telling what was going to fall out. I slipped her into pajamas and a robe, and went into the kitchen to start dinner. I opened the refrigerator and a harsh light glared at me. I looked inside the meat drawer: a round steak, breakfast sausages, hamburger, cheese, and more cheese.

I fried the sausages, cut planks of swiss cheese, and fixed two pickles on each plate. I made toast to make sandwiches. I scooted Mariko into her high chair, and we ate noisily, happy that we were home in spite of Carolyn's absence because there was something about the hour, the dusk settling in the streets, our neighbor raking leaves while other leaves were still coming down. I made another sandwich to share but left that one cold because we remembered the ice cream.

But our jaunty mood changed. After dinner Mariko stumbled on a throw rug, jamming a finger when she went down. I soaked her hurt under cold water as tears leapt from her eyes. I rocked her in my arms, cooing love words that quieted her so that she almost fell asleep. But she came back to life when I asked her if she wanted ice cream. I carried her to my bedroom, turned on the television to "Wild, Wild America," and went to the kitchen to measure ice cream into tumblers, seeing that most of everything was in the sink.

We watched her program, or tried to watch it because her demands grew: more napkins, a glass of water, a bigger Band-Aid for her finger, her stuffed dolphin in its homemade sleeping bag. I did a puppet show with her dolphin as the lead, but she was unmoved by my story of the motherless family with a barbaric deportment.

This was us, of course. Carolyn was gone, and the house, usually clean and steamy with kitchen smells, was a shock of strewn clothes, unwashed dishes, and odd smells that banged you out of nowhere.

After I put Mariko to bed, I began to pick up, but forgot all about my task when I found an article in *National Geographic* about otters so fascinating that I took it to bed with me immediately. The next morning, or what appeared to be morning, for it was still dark outside, Mariko shuffled in her slippers to my bed. She climbed in, asking about breakfast, and I was too tired, too out-of-it, to say a sentence to appease her hunger. When I opened an eye, she was sucking her thumb and running a tiny hand in my hair. She then moved a careful finger to my crusty eyes and peeled a few crumbs from the corners. I rolled over, groaned, and tried to stretch life into my body. I got up quickly, thinking perhaps that might do the trick. But it only made me dizzy. I fell back. I wrapped the blankets around my head and asked Mariko, "What if Mommy never comes back?"

Worry did something with her forehead. She stopped sucking her thumb, swallowed, and said, "I don't want to think about it." I didn't either. Someone had to save us. I shut my eyes but opened them wide to greet the new day. Mariko peeled more crust from the corner of my eyes and said that I was a dirty daddy.

Pets

OUR FIRST PET WAS BOOTS, AN ORANGE CAT WITH A TRI-angle-shaped head and teeth like a snake's, and who in fact became the snake of evilness when he ate Pete, our 25-cent canary from Woolworth's, a painted bird that dripped his artificial colors when he played in a tuna can of water. Pete faded right before our eyes, and seemed to chirp less and less, as if he himself had discovered that he was not exotic but just a plain yellow canary and no kin to the toucan or jungle-tree hummingbird. We liked him, nevertheless, especially when he gargled his seeds and jumped around in circles.

One evening Mom and we kids returned home to find the cage turned on its side, one bird's leg, twig-thin, on the floor, feathers floating in the air, and Boots on the dining table, blinking a set of satisfied eyes. The clues were in. Mom's eyes widened with anger as she swung at Boots. Poor cat, he went flying and, instead of on his feet, he landed on his head, scrambled, shrieked, and ran, literally, up the wall, almost touching the ceiling.

I liked Boots. She let us put flowers behind her ears and a paper cape on her back, and let us wrap her paws in aluminum foil so that she rustled when she walked. Space cat, we thought, she looks like she's from space. We were happy with ourselves, and crazy with laughter when we wrapped her entire body in aluminum. When she walked, she showered pieces of light and made a clinking sound like dragged chains. We were very sad when she died.

I liked Boots but liked our dog Blackie better, even though he would never allow us to wrap him in aluminum and play our space game. He had no special talent, except he was warm to hold. Being old, he slept mostly, drank water, moaned instead of barked, and wobbled when he trotted after us up the alley, thinking that perhaps we were leading him to food. He was the only dog we knew who liked raisins. That was his breakfast, and our breakfast too, with cereal or a buttered tortilla for us, and scraps for him. Raisins. They were free since our parents worked at Sun-Maid Raisins and they could bring boxes home as they pleased. Blackie also liked oranges and sometimes even dried apricots. Years later, when we got another dog and fed him fruit that he only looked at, I assumed he was ill and that he would go away like Pete and Boots and Blackie himself.

Blackie was hit by a car. My uncle was the first to find him and probe his belly and its bulb of blood. My brother and sister were there, with free pickles fished out of open barrels from the Coleman Pickle Company. It was summer, dusk, the west a pinkish streak where the sun went down. I didn't know about Blackie until Uncle had him in his arms and was carrying him down the alley where I waited for our Japenese neighbor to go inside so I could steal plums. But I forgot about the plums and joined the procession, petting Blackie's head and asking him if he was okay—did it hurt, did he want some raisins—and asking my uncle what he was going to do with Blackie. Uncle didn't say anything. We walked past the broom factory and its *wham wham* of machinery that tied straw to bright colorful sticks that became brooms.

We kids stopped at Van Ness and were told to stay there, to go home if we wanted, or wait, but not to dare cross the street because we might become like Blackie. Rick and Debra left in time, but I stayed and counted the *wham whams,* and thought that every four made one broom. That's a lot of brooms, I thought, more brooms than people. But soon I lost count and thought only of Blackie and where he was going. I was sad and scared, and wanted to cross the street but knew better. Uncle came back without our dog but with peaches. When I asked him where Blackie went, he said that he was living at another house with a happy family. Where, I asked, and he pointed, over there, and *there* was nothing but a dark outline of warehouses and poor houses, now that there was very little light.

I was four when we got him and six when we let him go. Father let me name him. I didn't know my colors very well at the time and chose Blackie, even though he was mostly brown like me and my brother and sister and the raisins that were in no way an afternoon snack but real food for the living.

Taking Notice

MARIKO IS SIX AND A HALF—OR SIX AND THREE QUARTERS, as she often says—and is thirty-nine inches tall. He hair is black; her eyes, slanted from a Japanese wind that's been blowing in my wife's family for 10,000 years, are brown and filled with light at almost any hour. She loves dresses and her stuffed animal, a dolphin the size of a hot dog, which she carries everywhere, even into sleep and watery dreams.

Her favorite holiday is Easter. There are things hiding in the grass—eggs and chocolates, a tiny gift to wear around her neck. Her favorite person is her mother. The second favorite person—herself. I'm number four, right behind our cat, Pip.

Mariko's a little philosopher in a starched jumper. After she jammed a finger against a chair and her mother told her that she should be more careful, she came back with, "How am I supposed to know the future!"

She's also blessed with tact. Once when we were stuck in traffic and her cousin was whining for this and that—Cokes, a restroom, more stick pretzels to smoke like cigarettes—she bent her five-year-old face to his four- year-old ear—and said in a whisper, "Diego, zip your lip."

Left handed. No scars. A little thin for a child who eats asparagus and artichokes, and everything else. The little space between her front teeth is marketable. When she smiles for the grandmothers, they fall over each other to open their purses and offer silver dollars for her bank.

Her greatest fear? Picking grapes. Her mother and I sometimes talk about that kind of work: the long hours, the wasps, the dust in the throat, the heat that won't go away. I say to her, "Mexicans are the people who pick grapes, and you're

Mexican, Ronnie [her nickname]." She plays with her food, worry darkening her brow, and then she looks up, hopeful: "I'm Japanese, too—they don't work that way, right, Mom?"

After school she reads, nibbles carrots for a snack, and follows her mother like a doctor from room to room. Since we have no other children, since there are no kids on our block, I often feel sorry for her, thinking she's missing out on something—friendship, fun, some fall from a tree that will help shape her character—and go out grudgingly to play a game with her, knowing that only nightfall or dinner will make her stop. On sunny days we stand in the backyard searching the flowery bushes for butterflies. I hold a homemade net; with two hands she grips a mayonnaise jar, with the lid off. We wait quietly for one to settle—poor creature that gets within range. I snap the net down, flick a yellow one into a mayonnaise jar, and later, at Mariko's insistence, pull off its wings to see what will happen. It always dies.

I'm taking notice. Today she's six and three-quarters, almost four-fifths, and already she's leaving us. She's putting on muscle and words and knowledge. Yesterday she came home with papers in her hands and said, "The vitamin C is in the skin of the grape, not the juice, Daddy." I didn't know that. And I didn't know how water runs uphill. She explained it to me with widened eyes and a flash of her tiny hands. I watched and listened, and would have given her everything in my heart, she was so sweet.

I'm a father and, like any father who's awake to his child, I can see her moving away. First it was her crawl, then steps, then words and whole sentences that have carried her this far. From a bloody cry on the mother's belly, she is now a little girl with colored pencils drawing her idea of what our house should look like. To her, we should have more trees—a ring of them making shadows everywhere. To her, we should add bedrooms where there is now an attic. We could see the bay from there. We're not far, she tells me. We're inching toward it each year—so say the scientists.

And summer this year? She swings like a lantern from the limbs of the apricot, and her arms color with the fruit. During the day, she's in love with the world from a plastic pool, and in the evening, her skin tingling from hours under the sun, she believes what she reads in bed. She's on her belly with her legs crossed in the air. I sit on the bed's edge to read to her. When she reads to me, I want to crawl into bed, tired from the day, and fall asleep to a story that always ends right.

She's almost seven. In another six years, she'll be as tall as her mother. Her skin will be a perpetual brown, the color of honey. Her body will be in bud: shoulders, breasts, the hip's curve like a mathematical equation that can't be solved. Her friends will be the same. They'll come over, quiet in my presence, in her mother's presence, but behind a closed bedroom door they'll laugh and gossip and share what there is to share in their thirteenth year.

I'm waiting for those years. I want to watch her play catch on the front lawn with a friend. They'll bend and stutter-step backwards. Their ponytails will ride the wind as they look skyward for a ball that will skip from their yapping mitts. I want to watch her sit among friends on the hood of my car. It will be summer when they talk about the nonsense of boys who won't go away. They'll giggle, roll their eyes, and cover their mouths to secrets that they'll half-remember a week later. They'll act big by themselves but small when they ask for money for an ice cream from a truck jingling up the street.

But I want the present, too, the little girl with scuffed knees and a stuffed dolphin. Let her tell me about vitamin C, dinosaurs, volcanoes, the Plains Indians. Let her ask me again and again for some sweet thing from the cupboard she can't reach. If there's nothing there, we can walk to the store. I take her hand for its tiny bell of warmth. At the corner, she asks, looking both ways and serious as she can get, "Now, Daddy?"

"Yes, Ronnie," I say, looking both ways myself. "Hold my hand tight. Don't let go." We'll hurry across, racing our shadows that seem so big that wherever we step is where we belong.

Evening Walk

WHENEVER I ANNOUNCE AFTER DINNER THAT WE'RE GOING for a walk my daughter runs to the back yard to busy herself with a handful of sand and leaves and things of that sort. I get up slowly from the couch, tired but knowing very well that a walk is what I need. I run a hand across my wife's rump as I pass her at the kitchen sink, dear wife elbow-deep in soap suds. She offers a quick cynical smile, as if to say, "You lazy bum, where are you going?"

The problem with an evening walk is that I talk a lot. I don't know when to be quiet. My daughter will start off at my side as together we admire gardens for what they are, alive or nearly alive with flowers, but half-way around the block and up Francis Street, she'll skip a few steps ahead because I will say things like, " That three is older than your grandma, but not by much. Did you know they put her in the concentration camp during the war, and Mommy would have had to go there too except Grandpa was fighting in Europe. I bet you didn't know that?"

In the back yard I find Mariko trying to piece together an apple that had fallen from the tree. She shows me the two halves. Strange, I think, I've never seen this happen—an apple split nearly perfectly in half. She tries to involve me in solving this phenomenon, and in fact I start talking about a baseball bat that once split right in two on a sissy hit to second base. Then I catch on; she's avoiding the walk.

"Let's go, kid," I tell her, and place the apple on a lawn chair, and together we start up the block around the corner and before you know I'm saying things like, "When I was a kid I picked grapes. Do you like grapes? Well it's a hard life cutting grapes. Hours and hours of work and the people who pick them don't get paid very much. My grandma used to do that kind of work, and my mom, and your uncles and aunt."

Mariko skips ahead with a branch she's picked up from the gutter. She doesn't want to hear it. I don't want to hear it either, but I think she has to know about difficult lives. She's a little girl with a piano and stuffed animals and three meals a day and snacks in fancy wrappers. Perhaps I'm an ogre about what I think is my duty, to explain the unjust world, just as when I tried to get her a head start on others by demanding that she know her colors just about the time she began to talk in sentences. I would pull up a handful of grass and ask, "What color?" *Green.* "And this?" pointing to the rose. "What color?" *Pink.* "My face?" *Brown.* "And my teeth?" tapping the front ones with a finger. *Orange.*

Darn kid, I remember laughing to myself. She's going to be a wise-guy.

I also thought it was my duty to tell her about Christ by saying a bed-time prayer. I didn't know that in the dark when I kissed her and she would say, "Kiss Dolphy too," her stuffed animal that she loves dearly, that she would turn him over and let me kiss his butt—or whatever it is that a dolphin has. She would laugh, and I thought it was out of happiness that she was discovering Christ.

Actually she's very sweet, shy to the point of rudeness, and doesn't need to be lectured to. She eats everything off her plate, prays, offers toys to friends because she loves them. She cries at movies and feels sorrow for characters in her books, and is eager to be held in our arms and would hold us—mommy and daddy—if she had the strength to pick us up.

Nevertheless, there's still that chance she'll grow up unappreciative. It's a father's duty to scare children out of their wits. "When I was a kid I fought Okies with my bare hands." I laugh at this one and she wrinkles her face, obviously disturbed that she should have to hear such trivia. "I sold pop bottles to buy my candy, and your uncle once broke his arm but didn't get to the doctor until we sold our furniture." I laugh at this, partly because it's true (my dumb brother dared Eddie King, a mean kid in a striped T-shirt, to run over his arm by lying on the sidewalk with an outstretched arm) and partly because I catch myself embroidering the past. Actually, we didn't have to sell our furniture, but we did wait a few days. Poor brother. That first night our mom tied two ice cubes in a wash cloth for his "hurt," closed the bedroom door on Rick to let him moan and cry, and let me taunt him for being a big baby.

"Some kids had to walk through snow," I tell her, hearing in the back of my head our stepfather, drunk at the kitchen table and repeating his stories. "Knew a kid who was picked up by a tornado, and a girl who was carried away by a pit bull. In my time, you had to be tough just to get to school."

When my story telling gets louder, Mariko begins to skip fast, not looking back, and I start walking faster, telling her about pickle barrels we stood in when we were kids. She's now running, the leafy stick in her hand fluttering like green-fire, because the corner is up ahead and an evening without me—and my stories—can't be far beyond.

THREE

Dining in Fresno

Yesterday, I drove the 180 miles from Berkeley to Fresno, my hometown, to visit my friend Jon Veinberg and talk with him about the super-eight movie we were planning about a sixties rock group to be called The Ministers of Love. In short, we were thinking of a comedy.

When I arrived it was late afternoon. We had a few beers in front of the TV, and toward dusk we left the house to have dinner at a Basque restaurant, Yturri. Since it was a weekday, business was slow. There was a young couple along the wall and two families with elbows on the table, waiting. Flies circled between the dining rooms.

The waitress hurried over, plucked two menus from the side of the cash register, and showed us to a table along the wall. We took a customary peek at the menu, although we both knew we were going to order deep-fried chicken. You couldn't beat the price; it was six-fifty for a five-course meal, with coffee and the choice of three kinds of ice cream to wash it all down.

We gave our orders, and soon dipped spoons into lentil soup and rowed for our lives. Scraped two kinds of salad onto our plates, vinegary lettuce and potato. Clunked chunks of stew onto our plates, green beans and garbanzo beans. Tore pieces of French bread we buttered entirely yellow, and talked and ate like Romans. We raised industrial-thick wine glasses to one another, slurped water, and sighed for the good life. When the chicken came, piled a foot high on a plate, I waved mine off and asked the waitress to bring me a doggie bag. She smiled and remarked,

"Big boys can't do it?"

"Whoa," said Jon, uncomfortably stuffed. I smiled, patted my belly like a trucker, and pushed my chair back.

We ordered coffee and were talking about friends when the obese family at one end of the long table in the middle of the room began to make faces at a skinny family who, in turn, soured their faces at the fatties. Finally, the oldest son of the fatties got up calmly, walked a few husky steps toward the other family, and ripped the cigarette out of the father's mouth.

"What the hell!" the father said in a restrained voice, getting halfway up, eye ragged with anger.

With a snicker on his face, the fat son returned to take his place with his family. His own father pretended nothing had happened while his mother, square box in a muu-muu, turned to one of her daughters, and muttered, "The guy can't even read. 'No smoking' sign right above his gourd. I swear."

"You better watch it, turkey," the father of the skinnies said, jabbing an angry finger. His face was pink and excited. "You hear me?" He stood glaring while his family—wife, two daughters, and his own son—played with their salad forks, eyes down, embarrassed. Finally the father sat down and picked up his fork.

Jon and I looked at one another, half-snickering.

"Did you see that?" I asked in a low voice. "Slapped that cigarette right out of his mouth."

Jon wagged his head. "I've been telling you for years, Fresno's crazy."

Both families began to mutter and throw ugly glances at each other. Finally the waitress asked the skinnies what the beef was. Pointing fingers sprang up like spears, followed by accusations and more pink faces. The waitress listened like a school teacher and disappeared into the kitchen to return with four liters of house wine—two for each family. She poured gurgling wine into stout wine glasses, which the adults gripped like clubs. Soon they returned to their meals and talk of work and daily matters, though occasionally one would steal a glance at the other family.

We finished our coffee, rolled ice from our water glasses in our mouths as we hoped something would happen, so we could step in and tell them to act like people, not wild animals. But nothing happened. Jon stubbed out his cigarette; I finished my wine. We left with our doggie bags, and instead of heading home right away we started to walk around the block to work off dinner.

It was a pleasant summer evening. The moon was a broken tooth hanging over the Fresno Ice Company; the wind was cool against our faces. What a life, I thought. We sauntered like tourists as we pointed out run-down houses, vacant lots, warehouses we'd love to give our names to. We were talking about a boarded-up machine shop when a squeaking Pinto full of black guys slowed to a stop in the middle of the street. We also slowed to a stop. They looked at us, the red coals of their cigarettes coming and going, and didn't say anything. I knew what this meant; if we continued walking they'd jump us for the three or four dollars in Jon's wallet, and the twenties in mine. Without looking at one another, Jon and I turned around, took a few nonchalant steps, but hurried away when they called us to help push-start their car, an old trick I myself had used in high school. We ran back to the neon glare of the restaurant—ran because we loved our faces as they were, not bloodied or pounded like first-grade clay.

We stood at the entrance, hands on hips, and waited to catch our breath. Jon said, "You're lucky that you live in Berkeley. There ain't a damn thing to do in this town, except get beat up."

This was true. In Berkeley you could go to the symphony, maybe a poetry reading, or a foreign movie. You could take in the evening and return home alive. In Fresno, once rated the worst city in the United States by the Rand-McNally Report, you could go out for dinner and later be thrown from a speeding car, quite dead.

We went back inside hoping the skinnies and fatties were so drowned in house wine that when they saw us, blurry friends of the same dinner, they would motion us over to choose sides and fight for the simple thrill of being alive.

The Concert

ONCE IN MEXICO CITY AND TIRED OF ITS NOISE AND rushed people, my wife and I flew to Oaxaca, a city known for its pottery, weavings, and the nearby ruins of Monte Alban and Mitla. We stayed in a hotel whose courtyard was sheltered by a huge skylight that let in a hazy, almost silver light. For two days we took buses to the ruins, bought Mexican toys, and walked from one end of the town to the other in search of out-of-the-way shops.

On our last night we went to hear the National Symphony. I bought low-priced tickets but when we tried to sit on the ground floor, a portly usher pointed us to the stairwell. We climbed to the next landing where another usher told us to keep climbing by rolling his eyes toward *el paraíso*—the gallery of cheap seats. We climbed two more flights, laughing that we were going to end up on the roof with the pigeons. An unsmiling usher handed us programs as we stepped to the door. We looked around, amazed at the gray, well-painted boxes that were our seats. There were no crushed velvet chairs with ornate wooden arms, no elegant men and women with perfect teeth. Most were Indians and campesinos, and a few university students holding hands, heads pressed together in love.

I led Carolyn to the boxes in the front row against the rail and together we looked far down where the others sat. Their rumblings rose like heat. They fanned themselves and smiled wide enough for us to see their teeth. We watched them until an old man touched my shoulder, said *con permiso*, and took small steps to get past me to the box on our left. When he sat down I smiled at him as I wanted to be friendly. But he didn't look at me. He took out a pair of glasses from his breast pocket. They were broken, taped together at the bridge. I looked away, embarrassed to see that he was poor, but stole a glance when the program began: I saw his coat, slack and full from wear, and his pants with oily spots. His shoes were rope sandals. His tie was short, like a withered arm. I watched his face in profile that showed a knot of tape protruding from his glasses; a profile that went unchanged as it looked down at the symphony.

I listened but felt little as the violins tugged and pulled and scratched through an hour of performance. When the music stopped and the conductor turned around, moon-faced and trying to hide his happiness by holding back a grin, I craned my neck over the rail and watched the *elegantes* applaud and smile at one another. We applauded, too, and looked around, smiling. We were busy with an excitement that lit our eyes. But while the *elegantes* got up to take drinks and stand in the foyer under torches, those around us leaned against the wall to smoke and talk in whispers. A group of young men played cards and, in a sudden win, laughed so hard that the usher came over to quiet them down.

We stayed for the second half—something by Haydn—but no matter how I tried to study the movements of musicians and conductor on his carpeted box, I couldn't help but look around the room at the Indians and campesinos whose faces, turned in profile in the half-lit shadows, held an instinctive awareness of the music. They would scratch a cheek or an elbow, speak quietly to one another, and sometimes squirm on the boxes. But most were attentive. It amazed me. I had never known the poor to appreciate such music, and I had lived among the poor since I was a child. These field laborers and rug weavers listened to music that was not part of their lives, music written to titillate the aristocrats who wanted so much to rise above the dirty faces of the poor. The poor sat on the fifth tier on painted boxes, bodies leaning in the direction of the music that couldn't arrive fast enough to meet their lives.

When the concert ended, the old man next to me stood up and asked for permission to pass. I pinched my knees together and Carolyn stood up. She sat back down and together, heads touching like lovers, we looked down to the first floor where the *elegantes* chatted with drinks and fluttery fans, and shook each other's hands as if celebrating their wealth.

After a while we got up and, with campesinos who were talking about a recently read book, descended the four flights to the ground.

Canary, Cat, and Dog

AT TIMES THE DAYS ARE SO QUIET, SO HARMLESS, THAT I could welcome a canary into our home—a canary with its rusty squeak and its nervous shifting from perch to perch. I welcome this bird. It taps its tiny bell, gargles seed, and looks over its shoulder like a poet into a mirror. "Paco, here's my finger"—and it flutters its wings, makes noises, and pokes with its trumpet of a beak. His bite doesn't hurt, just stings like bad medicine.

If not a canary, then I welcome a cat who's a furry thing from a wet road. I want to come home from school to find an orange one licking its bristle brush of a paw at my doorstep, a cat that raises its three-cornered head and gives me a "what's-there-to-eat" look. I step inside, put down my books, and yank open the refrigerator, the white light coming on.

"Cheese," I say, "there's cheese and olives and meats—and milk for your goofy face."

I fix a plate for the cat and together we sit by the fireplace, yellow from a few fired-up sticks and rolled newspapers. I offer the day's events, but the cat doesn't look up, only bobs and weaves its head over each bite. If it looks up, it is to see that I keep my distance, keep my sneaky hand away from the drumstick.

If not a canary or cat, then I welcome a dog who can walk briskly and purposefully down any mean street. Black, brown, black and brown—it's all the same to me. I welcome a street dog, fur like a wet rake. A dog who has stared into garbage cans and sniffed what was best. When I was a kid I owned a lost dog for a day. That day we walked together in alleys to search trees for fruit and peek into trash bins where we found tuna cans licked clean as cats. If I pulled out a light bulb to rattle a made-up song, the dog with dancing feet yanked out a soup can. He gripped it between his paws and lapped it until his tongue got tired, if not bloody. He looked around with his twitching nose in the air. Birds crossed up the sky; smoke rode on the wind. He twitched his nose, then lowered it back into the can for a final lick.

Yesterday on campus while on the way to class, I saw a mangy dog who had eaten egg shells in his lifetime. He was crouched behind a bench, tongue hanging and breathing hard. He looked at me and I looked at him and we almost recognized one another. If he could have talked, he would have held my stare and said, "Get over here! I know who you are."

And if I were less smart, I would sit on the bench and let him, a remembering dog, sniff my hand. "You're Mexican," he says. "What are you doing here, guy?"

"Teaching."

"Teaching, my foot! Chasing free lunches is more like it, sucker."

"Quiet," I say, embarrassed that my past has come back like a lost child. "Someone will hear."

Students. Professors with tenure votes. Young women in dresses like skimpy clouds. I look around, scared as a dunked cat, and tell him that things have changed—that I am an assistant professor, that I am reading almost great books, that I am thinking about Europe for the summer.

"You ain't thinking a damn thing," the dog says. He rises to his feet, stiffly. "I know who you are, so listen up."

And I do. I take his order: a sandwich, make that two, and a length of bologna still in its plastic wrapper. And water. And a flea collar. And dog eyedrops if they have them because he's been up all night looking for a good time. I go and come back because he's my kin, blood brother to bad days.

If he were smarter, and I less smart, there would be no choice. The alleys would call—the rich harvest of everything discarded and rank in the sun—and I would have to go because we are friends to the same past that won't lie down and die for good.

The Young Poet Under a Tree

LARRY WAS A COLLEGE FRIEND WHO LIVED UNDER A TREE. I would see him on campus with a book thin as a sandwich in his hand, or walking to a busy corner to hitchhike God knows where. He took me to his tree one day and together, on weeds flattened into a dusty carpet, we sat and talked, mostly about books we had read—Rimbaud and Hamsun—and sometimes about our poetry. I recall a poem of his about an Egyptian cat whose eyes were many-cornered diamonds. After a while he poured me a cup of water and measured a handful of seeds into my palms. They were unsalted, bland as paper, but I popped them into my mouth, one by one, while I talked about important books and the poems I wanted to write.

When our conversation stalled I got up and said that I had to leave. He got up also, asking me to wait because he wanted to give me something. When he turned his back, I looked around: his sleeping bag was rolled loosely and propped against the tree; a cardboard box showed cans of soup and tuna; a desk, with a scatter of fallen leaves, stood in sunlight. Larry hovered over it as he felt inside a drawer. He turned to me with a sheaf of lined paper—poems, I realized. He gave them to me to read, to have.

I left thinking how sad it was not to live in a house, and walked to my girlfriend's apartment, which was not more than twenty yards from the tree. Carolyn was on the front porch watering her spring plants from a milk carton. Yellow things yawned their brightness; carnations were nodding their ruffled heads in the noontime breeze. When I called to her, she looked up with a flash of happiness in her eyes. She hugged me with one arm, that first love of three weeks, and led me inside her apartment to make me a sandwich that I nibbled, fish-like, until it was only crumbs on a paper plate. After I finished a bowl of ice cream, we went outside, arm in arm, to sit on the front steps. But startled, I got up as I remembered Larry's poems. I went inside and returned to read them to Carolyn—poems about ancient learning, Greece, astrological signs. None of them made sense, though neither one of us let on that we didn't understand them. "He's very ambitious," I finally said after minutes of silence. Carolyn nodded her head. She took the poems and placed them face down, then asked me who had written them. I took her by the hand and led her to the back of her apartment where I pointed to a cluster of trees: feathery smoke and faint guitar-playing in the air.

"There's nothing over there," she said. Shushing her, I said that Larry the poet lived under a tree. She furrowed her brow and clicked her tongue, calling me "silly lover boy." She let go my hand and walked toward the tree to see for herself only to return, head down and troubled as she hurried back to her apartment where she threw herself on the bed and told me to go home. I cooed words into her ear, petting her hair and massaging her shoulders as I tried to perk her up. Not knowing what to do, I told her, however lamely, that someone had to be poor. I bit the back of my hand, realizing how stupid it sounded, and got off the bed to look out the window: smoke rose not in a feathery column but in huge, cheeky puffs. His guitar was noisier, his southern was voice louder. I imagined him sitting on a box while his big shoe tapped quietly to his playing. The poor were so close, so real, that you could close your eyes and see them anytime.

The Man on the Floor

YESTERDAY MORNING MY WIFE AND I WORKED UP THE ground for spring planting. This was something new for us— a garden we could see from the kitchen window. Ferns and begonias would go along the fence and, farther back, near the fig tree where there was more sun, would grow tomatoes, chiles, and maybe eggplant, those lopsided heads I disliked as a kid but love now.

While I shoveled, my wife shook out grassy roots and wild onion that she piled like wet laundry. At first we worked talking about our new house: how we would panel the bathroom with redwood and put in a greenhouse window. But as the rhythm of shovel-and-pull sped up, we worked quietly side by side, bent over and occasionally grunting from fatigue or a tough root. And even though it was cold, the sun gleamed behind clouds. Sweat moistened my face from the push and tug of shovel work. I wanted to take off my flannel shirt, but my wife said that I would catch cold. Even our daughter, who was waist-high in a pile of leaves, was warm, her face pink from sucking a thumb. She raised many leaves to us, and each time we had to act surprised and open our mouths wide to say "Wow!"

We shoveled and pulled and leveled the ground with a rake. Afterwards we went inside to rest. But I couldn't stay. I had a meeting with students at 12:30. I drove and parked off campus, near Telegraph Avenue, and since I was early I went to Giant Hamburger to get something to eat. I was in line thinking about the garden when the man in front of me slugged the waitress who was taking his order. The blow pushed her back against the Coke machine, and a bright string of blood spilled from her mouth to her apron. My mind is not working, I thought. This can't be happening.

I saw the man's face twist with ugliness. I heard him yell, "You white bitch," and saw him pick up a pot of coffee. I heard myself think, "Grab him," and I did, in a sort of bear hug. He let go of the pot and, as he tried to wrestle free from my hold, I picked him up, pushed my weight on his, and together we went down to the floor—a high-school wrestling move that was more instinct than thought.

I took him down and used my weight, my chin in his back, an occasional head slap, to keep him down as one of the workers called the police. But he was strong and crawled, snail-like, calling, "You white mutherfucker, I'm going to kill you!" He said it repeatedly with such rage that I began to believe him, especially when, in spite of my hold, he started to rise to his knees. I pounded one of his arms from under him, so that he collapsed like a table. He shouted names, and I shouted back, "Mutherfucker, you ain't going to do shit!" I shouted until I was in a rage, like a chain saw dropped on the ground and dancing with fury. I hit him in the face, in the back, in the face again and even spat at him.

When he started to get up again, I looked to the customers who remained in the restaurant, some of whom were munching hamburgers and lapping up chips. "You guys better help me if this guy gets up," I said in a desperate voice, because I knew I was in trouble if he should reverse holds. But they looked at me dully and unmoved, and I was scared. I could hear the waitress sob and a worker talking to his boss on the phone. Another stood with a towel over his shoulder. I looked at him and he looked at me. Everything seemed heightened, like a movie seen too close to the screen.

What amazed me is that some people came into the restaurant but seeing us on the ground immediately turned to flee. There were those who came in, looked down at us as they walked to the counter, and tried to place an order, as if this were a common occurrence, as if Mexicans and black men often wrestle in restaurants.

When the police arrived, I let go and moved away so the black man wouldn't see my face. I didn't want him to know who I was or what color I was. I went into the back room where the waitress was sitting on a keg of beer, eyes still red from crying. She thanked me and I said it was nothing. She got up and from her jeans pulled out coupons for free hamburgers. "Come in anytime, and you order what you want," she offered. When a cop came in with a clipboard, I left the back room to a "thank you." She smiled and her teeth were fringed with blood.

I was leaving when one of the workers handed me a bag of burgers and fries, and another bag of Cokes. I thanked him and walked up the street a little tense, a little shaky, but only a half hour late to my meeting.

To Be a Man

HOW STRANGE IT IS TO CONSIDER THE DISHEVELED MAN sprawled out against a store front with the rustling noise of newspaper in his lap. Although we see him from our cars and say "poor guy," we keep speeding toward jobs, careers, and people who will open our wallets, however wide, to stuff them with money.

I wanted to be that man when I was a kid of ten or so, and told Mother how I wanted my life. She stood at the stove staring down at me, eyes narrowed, and said I didn't know what I was talking about. She buttered a tortilla, rolled it fat as a telescope, and told me to eat it outside. While I tore into my before-dinner snack, I shook my head at my mother because I knew what it was all about. Earlier in the week (and the week before), I had pulled a lawn mower, block after block, in search of work. I earned a few quarters, but more often screen doors slapped shut with an "I'm sorry," or milky stares scared me to the next house.

I pulled my lawn mower into the housing projects that were a block from where we lived. A heavy woman, with veined legs and jowls like a fat purse, said, "Boy, you in the wrong place. We poor here."

It struck me like a ball. They were poor, but I didn't even recognize them. I left the projects and tried houses with little luck, and began to wonder if they too housed the poor. If they did, I thought, then where were the rich? I walked for blocks, asking at messy houses until I was so far from home I was lost.

That day I decided to become a hobo. If it was that difficult pulling quarters from a closed hand, it would be even more difficult plucking dollars from greedy pockets. I wanted to give up, to be a nobody in thrown-away clothes, because it was too much work to be a man. I looked at my stepfather who was beaten from work, from the seventeen years that he hunched over a conveyor belt, stuffing boxes with paperback books that ran down the belt quick as rats. Home from work, he sat in his oily chair with his eyes unmoved by television, by the kids, by his wife in the kitchen beating a round steak with a mallet. He sat dazed by hard labor and bitterness yellowed his face. If his hands could have spoken to him, they would have asked to die. They were tired, bleeding like hearts from the inside.

I couldn't do the same: work like a man. I knew I had the strength to wake from an alley, walk, and eat little. I knew I could give away the life that the television asked me to believe in, and live on fruit trees and the watery soup of the Mission.

But my ambition—that little screen in the mind with good movies—projected me as a priest, then a baseball coach, then a priest again, until here I am now raking a cracker across a cheesy dip at a faculty cocktail party. I'm looking the part and living well—the car, the house, and the suits in the closet. Some days this is where I want to be. On other days I want out, such as the day I was in a committee meeting among PhDs. In an odd moment I saw them as pieces of talking meat and, like meat we pick up to examine closely at supermarkets, they were soul-less, dead, and fixed with marked prices. I watched their mouths move up and down with busy words that did not con-nect. As they finished mouthing one sentence to start on another, they just made up words removed from their feelings.

It's been twenty years since I went door to door. Now I am living this other life that seems a dream. How did I get here? What line on my palm arched into a small fortune? I sit before students, before grade books, before other professors talking about books they've yet to write, so surprised that I'm far from that man on the sidewalk, but not so far that he couldn't wake up one day, walk a few pissy steps saying, "It's time," and embrace me for life.

This Is Who We Are

THIS PAST DECEMBER WHILE ON MY WAY TO FRESNO FOR Christmas, I picked up two hitchhikers in Modesto. Usually I won't stop; usually I only have time to glance at a sleeve or a blackened knee or a creased face, not the whole man, before I press the gas pedal to get the car going faster. Call it guilt, call it common sense—a quick knife along the throat could end all dreams. Still when I see someone on the side of the road, I press the pedal and turn up the radio so my guilt can't hear itself.

In the early seventies, when I was a college student, I hitch-hiked up and down California, especially Highway 99, that black snake that runs through the valley—Sacramento, Modesto, Turlock, Madera, Fresno, Tulare, Delano, and Bakersfield. I kicked cans along my way, hid behind cows when the police crept on frontage roads, and felt so cut off from school and family that I was another person. In Strathmore, a trucker going a different way let me off. I thanked him, shrugging my backpack onto my shoulder, and for ten miles walked without caring if I flagged down a ride. The openness fascinated me. The sky, with a flap of geese angling south, was ash-color. Sparrows bickered on wire fences; cattle looked dully at the ground, drooling. The fields were brown in front of me but gray-black in the distance where the coastal range began. I walked in wonder at the quiet, at the absence of people, their voices and all their whining. I wondered at how simple it would be to lie in the grass and stay there until I looked like the grass—green, wet, and part of the world. But I went on and, by nightfall, I was in San Luis Obispo eating hamburgers with a friend in a makeshift tent.

I recall hitchhiking with others from Newhall, a suburb outside the San Fernando Valley, and being grateful that a truck had stopped, that the driver was human enough to recognize we were freezing among islands of snow turning to slush under the rain. There were five of us at the freeway entrance but room for only three in the cab. With another, I volunteered to get in the bed of the truck. I had been cold on the side of the road but was colder as the truck climbed the mountains on the way to Tehachapi and the quick descent into the Central Valley. Wind whipped our faces, making us shudder and beg the driver to pull over and let us ride in the cab for a while. But the driver, a grandfather in a plaid hunting jacket, didn't bother to look over his shoulder to see how we were doing. He was talking with everything he had— mouth, hands, brow that went up and down with lines—to the three in the cab, who were nodding their heads in agreement to whatever he was saying. When we finally stopped to let off two in Bakersfield, I was stiff from the rain and my hands were red, as if a flashlight were shining from behind them. I and the other person in the back hopped into the cab, thankful for the bell of warmth from the heater. The driver smiled at us; his eyes were glassy as if he had been drinking. He shifted gears and soon we were speeding past McFarland, Pixley, Delano, and the small towns of hard labor. He talked about Jesus and the sins of the world. Near Fowler the grandfather said that we hitchhikers could kill him and he wouldn't care. Jesus was on his side. Jesus would know everything. I hunched in my coat, occasionally peeking at the grandfather who wouldn't stop. I nodded my head to his talk and counted the miles to Fresno. This was a crazy man behind the wheel, a highway evangelist with us as his followers. We didn't bother to tell him to shut up even though he was a madman because we were grateful that he had saved us from the cold.

That was ten years ago when I was twenty-one. Last

December I picked up two hitchhikers: one was, as he said, a bum, and the other was a private in the Army Reserve. The soldier, who was out of uniform, had come from a town outside Seattle hoping to reach El Paso by Christmas. He was broke, or nearly broke. When he had been discharged from basic training a month before, he took a bus to his hometown where he, a proud eighteen-year-old man, gave his mother $300. She bought groceries and booze, and after they were gone she told him to get a job. When he couldn't find one, she told him to get out. He left with bad words. Two days later he was in California, in my car with a bum and a college professor who was failing at tenure.

And the bum? He was shivering when I picked him up, not from the cold but from a fever. He had spent the night at the freeway entrance, praying in the dark that someone would stop. But no one did. He was too ragged to trust. His face was a smear of dirty Vaseline; his coat was coming apart at the sleeves. When he got in, I could smell the stink of his unwashed clothes. The private could smell him too. But we pretended everything was okay, that he didn't have a fever and that he wasn't as poor as you can get without dying. I offered the two oranges and a sandwich, which they tore in half, thanking me three or four times. At first few words were exchanged, perhaps because they were tired or perhaps we didn't know how to begin. But by the time we were coming into Turlock, the bum was telling stories, from the easy days in Oklahoma City where he had worked as a bricklayer and had a house and family, to the bad year in San Quentin because he had "messed up" a friend for stealing his television.

"I just went crazy," he said. "I found him and beat him with a clock, an iron one. "Looked like a wagon wheel."

He then quieted without telling us what had happened to him afterwards. He stared out the window to the fields that ran along Highway 99. A few minutes later, he was telling us how he and a buddy were jailed in a town outside Redlands in Southern California. They had been driving from Pomona to Needles in search of work and, tired from not sleeping the night before, had pulled to the side of the road to curl up for a couple of hours.

"It was hot, so I took off my shirt and shoes," he said. And we were just sleeping when a cop was looking at us and saying we were drunk. But we weren't. We didn't have money to buy nothing."

He was arrested and released an hour later, though his friend remained jailed. When he asked for his shirt and shoes, the policeman pushed him out the door into the daylight that had the bum squinting like a criminal. The policeman went around the back of the police department and returned with a piece of cardboard the size of a surfboard. "These are your shoes, Okie," he said, flinging it at him. "Get your ass moving. Move!"

The bum described how it was so hot—110 degrees or hotter—that he couldn't take more than a dozen steps before he had to drop the cardboard and step on it, feet stinging like a hard slap. For two miles to the freeway, he ran, dropped the cardboard and stood there until his feet cooled. He did it over and over. He did it while kids jeered on bicycles; while teenagers spit from their daddies' cars; while families in station wagons flicked balled ice cream wrappers at him. At the freeway entrance, he hunkered all afternoon, hurting for water and a cool place to sit as he waited for a car that finally stopped, eighteen hours later. The driver, a rancher from Oxnard, bought him burgers and Cokes, and in Redlands let him pick out shoes and a shirt at a thrift shop. He gave him two dollars and was gone.

He told other stories until I couldn't stand them and opened my own mouth to keep from hearing any more. I looked at him as I talked. His face—his eyes, his teeth—was used. He was shaking like a struck dog, this man with no luck to save himself. His life was over but the flesh went on, with the little memories of hope. I looked at the private in the rear-view mirror and he looked at me with eyes the color of river rock. He knew, I knew—this man was hurting. There was nothing we could do for him.

I pulled off in Madera to let the bum off. He thanked me without looking at me and trotted across a plot of freeway ivy toward an intersection. The private hopped in the front seat and for thirty miles to Fresno we said very little. He stared at the fields and commercial buildings—tire shops and farm equipment—in search of something to keep his mind busy. I was thinking of the words that had stung me. "The poorer you get, the more people think you look dead. And dead people don't need a damn thing."

I let the private off at a gas station in Fresno and drove to my in-laws for Christmas dinner, hoping that it wasn't true: the poor are like the dead, with little air space and no room to move.

Expecting Friends

MY FRIENDS ARE COMING—JON THE ESTONIAN AND OMAR
the Mexican—and what we want is to sit under the apricot tree
in the backyard and talk about friends who couldn't come—
Chris the one-book scholar and Leonard the two-beat drum-
mer. We're going to talk poetry, ours mostly, and open beers
one after another until we're a little drunk and a little wiser
than the chairs we're sitting on. But we're going to take this
slowly. We may, in fact, not sit under that tree but first take a
drive to Tilden Park, where we'll hike as if there's a place to go
and maybe sit waist-deep in wild grass, chewing long stalks that
are springboards for the ants. Later we could go the Country
Club and slouch in leather chairs that overlook the green and
its small rise of hills. Men in plaid kneeling over golf balls.
Clouds over the trees. Trees like pieces of the sea standing up.
The day will be so open, so filled with blue air, that we won't
believe it's all for us.

But who are these friends? Jon was a classmate in poetry,
roommate in Laguna Beach, and the best man in my wedding, a guy who drank to all the causes of the heart. A friend
writes of Jon and the day of the wedding:

> The best man, lifting
> at least his fifth bottle of champagne,
> stands on a table in his white tuxedo;
> and turning slowly toward us, like Tommy Dorsey
> to the band, invites us to toast the moon,
> the clear Fresno moon, which he finds gone.

And the moon did disappear, for my wife and I married

on a night of an eclipse that comes every twenty years, a rare treat for the astronomer's wife. We didn't know. We planned the wedding from an old calendar, sent out homemade invitations, and stood in front of a churchroom of relatives who gave money, clock radios, vases, a quilt, and a new bed to wear down over the years. Here are sensible gifts, they were saying. Now make a home. Make a laughing baby in your arms.

And Omar? He was already a poet when I was a naive college student who carried books under both arms when we first met in a hallway at Fresno State in 1972. I put down my books and asked, "Are you really Omar?" He smiled, offered a clammy hand, and said, "Keep reading, young man," when I told him how much I admired his poetry. And I did. I read lines like, "Someone is chasing me up my sleeve" and "If I remember the dying maybe I'll be all right."

Later in the year I saw him with friends in front of the student union. Omar looked tattered, like a sailor roughed up by the sea, for his face was stubbled, his eyes red and milky in the corners, and his hair stiff as a shirt collar. I joined him and his friends who were hunched in old trench coats, feet moving a little because it was a gray December. No one was talking or about to talk. They looked around like sparrows, heads turning nervously left and then right, and shivered the cold from their shoulders. I looked around too and shivered, shaking off the cold. Trying to be friendly, I asked Omar how he was doing. He turned to me with a crazed look and said, "Go ask the dead!" I was taken back, surprised by his tone and half-eclipsed eye. Then he relaxed and chuckled; his friends chuckled. I opened my mouth into a stiff smile, stood with them for a while longer, and finally said goodbye as I hurried away with my sophomore books under my arms.

Omar the Crazy Gypsy, Lord Byron in Mexican clothes,

cheerleader of the acid set of the late sixties, is now a quiet poet in the rural town of Sanger where, on weekends with an uncle, he sells pants, shirts, cowboy hats, and whatever workers buy from the back of a station wagon or sweaty tents at swap meets. He is a merchant, he says, and when I ask jokingly if he sells his poetry too, he says, "Yes, they cost too. Right here." He touches his heart, and I know what he means.

These friends are coming to visit. We may drive to Tilden Park; we may drive across the San Rafael Bridge and search the water for migrating whales through binoculars. We'll pass the C&H Sugar Refinery in Crockett, then San Quentin, and finally come to the moss-green hills of Sonoma. We'll drive talking and looking left, then right, between bites of apples and slapped-together sandwiches. We may stop to take pictures of cows; we may stop at a roadside bar with a name like The South Forty or The Trail's End and stand drinking frosty beers. After a beer or two we may become so at ease that we invite a cowpoke who, after two or three or four beers, may call us city queers and hit us on our silly grins.

If we were smart we'd only drink one beer and get out—or just stay home, my home in Berkeley, under that apricot tree in the feathery light of an early spring day. The world is in blossom: apple and apricot, the tulip and yellow daffodil that is broken by wind. The sky is like no other: blue over the garage and silver-blue where the sun is coming through behind a rack of clouds. The breeze is doing things in the trees; my neighbor's dog is wagging his tail against the fence.

This will be Saturday. I will get my winter wish: to sit with friends who mean much to me and talk about others who mean much to us. I've been waiting for this moment. I've been waiting months to open up to others, laugh, and flick beer tops at kidding friends who have drunk too much. We'll carry chairs from the kitchen and set them under the tree. My wife may join us; I'll slap my lap and she'll sit with a sparkling wine glass in her hand. And our daughter may come out with her flying dolphin, a stuffed animal that's taped together and just hanging on. This will be Saturday, the weather faintly remembered from another time. In the backyard we may talk, or not talk, but be understood all the same.

Pulling a Cart

I REMEMBER A MAN IN OVERALLS WITH A ROPE OVER HIS shoulder, weight slanting like a rickety fence, pulling a wooden cart onto our street. In the cart a woman sat queen-like, swaddled in bulky sweaters and two or three skirts the color of clay. Her face was also clay-colored: bitten face of hard years, an unlit pipe cold in her hanging mouth. Husband and wife, they rattled our way in search of paper and glass, broken clocks and radios, heads of lettuce from garbage cans that we set on the curb on Wednesdays. Fruit beckoned them into our yards. Figs filled their hands and oranges bobbed on high limbs. They camped in alleys, lit small stick-crossed fires, and slept under trees. If it was winter and raining, they pulled a tarp over their heads, hunched together sitting up, and blinked like birds all through the night.

But they turned onto our street only in summer, it seemed. If we were inside, we kids looked on sadly from the front windows. If we were outside, we half-hid behind the bushes or skinny trees to watch them pass. They didn't bother to look around. The husband faced the next street, indifferent to the neighbors peeking from behind curtains, and the wife, shadow-filled face down, played with a handkerchief. After they passed we came out from hiding to watch the cart rattle to the next block. They left and we went on playing.

Husband and wife. That is what they were, living a poverty that scared even the poor. And on our street, a Mexican street with a few Okie faces, we knew better than to taunt or point or feel ashamed of the ragged. We were scared for them and, in a real way, we were scared for ourselves because one day we might have to pull a cart with a woman bundled in so many clothes that we wouldn't know where the cloth ended and the flesh began.

But as I grew older I became less shocked by their presence in my life. I remember when I saw them on the Fresno Mall. A girl and I were eating popcorn and sharing a Coke when a noise started toward us. I looked up. It was them: clay-colored and bundled deeper in rags. On that Saturday, I was in love and trying to be a man of thirteen with two girlfriends already behind me. When I saw the cart making its way toward us, I made a sour face because they were ruining everything. It was a spring day. I was in love. I had money to buy popcorn and a Coke, and the girl liked me enough to play with my sleeve. But they still came, the cart rattling so loudly on its skates that I momentarily lost that feeling of love, and forgot the girl and the popcorn and the Coke that was by then a rattle of ice in a cup. I looked away. I felt soiled to see them. When they finally disappeared around a corner, love wasn't them same. We pinched crumbs from the popcorn bag. We scattered some for the sparrows who bickered at our feet, like husbands and wives.

I won't be like them, I thought then, twenty years ago when I was a little man with a pretty date. Now I wonder. My wife is not centered on that cart; our daughter is not trailing us, vacant-eyed and hungry. No one is gawking; no one is pointing out our sadness when we take walks in the evening. But some days I feel as if I'm pulling a cart. My hands are frayed; the rope is frayed. The jars we collect along the way jingle like strange music and the newspapers, stacked and bundled, rustle in the wind of my pulling.

Some days my wife feels she's pulling me, in our tenth year of marriage, and no doubt our daughter, in her sixth year, feels that her pull keeps us together. We're making our way up this street, then that street. It's an effort that seems to take us no closer to what we want. The days end; dusk settles in the street. We never arrive.

Others are married, doing the same. They are pulling carts, weighed down with problems and finding no end in each step. It amazes me. I would think more would drop that rope and clop away in unlaced shoes, not looking back. But half of us stay, even if life is a pocketful of change, a cart, an apple and its bruised heart. We believe what we believe, and stay where we are.

Poor husband and poorer wife. I am amazed that we can be so human for only what we hold in our arms.

Ziggy

HE WANTED TO SHOW ME SOMETHING, THIS OLD Confederate son in three sweaters who lived in the same four-cottage complex as my wife and I, a just-married couple settling in with a few sticks of furniture, a kitchen full of wedding gifts, and a new bed that made a *hush* sound when we sat on it. His name was Ziggy, and he was old, a drunk perhaps, and so bored that he even bored me when he passed with a coffee can of water to sprinkle on the drive where no cars parked.

"What is it?" I asked. "Is it the squash?"

"No."

"Did the melon crack?"

"No, no."

My wife's lucky, I thought. She's at work. She doesn't know the pain of looking at Ziggy's vegetable garden each day; he bends down and shows me the underside of a green-going-to-red tomato. He squashes worms between his fingers, wipes his hands on his Can't-Bust-'Em jeans, and thinks nothing of it.

"Well, what is it?" I asked. "Is it about the mail?"

At least once a week he showed me a piece of misdirected mail for people who had lived in the complex. Some were dead, others moved away, some in the poorhouse like Hank Betzina, who didn't know what to do when his wife died. He shared the stories behind the names, and I, not wanting to be rude, feigned interest and even asked questions. What he did with that mail I never asked.

That morning he had something else for me. He snorted and cleared his throat. He started toward his cottage, an age-peppered hand beckoning me to follow. And I did. I wiped my shoes at his doormat, the letters of welcome nearly rubbed

off, and walked in sniffing the air because it smelled of cabbage, or something like cabbage. A quiet fly circled a bare
lightbulb in the kitchen.

Ziggy laughed. He asked how old I was. I told him I was
twenty-three, and he said he was sixty-eight but felt like a mil-
lion-year-old wharf rat. He laughed, then wiped his hand
across his face and took two steps to the wall, which he slapped
with an open palm. The floor began to move—herds of startled cockroaches clicked against each other as they raced from
under the couch and armchair.

I stepped back and made an ugly face. Jesus Christ, I
thought, and "Jesus Christ," I said as I started toward the door
to get the hell out. Ziggy laughed, held my shoulder.

"It's just a joke, boy."

"It's more than a joke," I said, peeling his fingers from my
shoulder. "It's sick."

Some cockroaches raced into the hallway that led to his
bedroom, but most made off to the kitchen, where they hid
behind stacks of newspapers and under the water heater and
the sink, where the garbage was kept. His apartment once
again became very still. The alarm clock buzzed its electronic
time and the oscillating fan rattled the newspapers strewn on
the coffee table. Ziggy raised a finger before his pursed lips
and said, "Shush." He tip-toed in his huge engineer boots to
the kitchen and looked over his shoulder at me, his mouth
slowly opening to reveal the broken-down fence of gray teeth.
He slowly turned his head back around, then jumped as old
people jump, stiffly and only a few inches off the floor but
high enough to come down and scare the cockroaches back
into action. They swarmed from hiding, and Ziggy, quick for
an old guy, his eyes shiny with crazed happiness, stepped on as
many as he could. He yelled for me to help him, and I just
stepped back, horrified. I felt one under my shoe, and still
another. I imagined the cockroach thinning to a gray paste

under my shoes, and imagined that Ziggy was a year or so away from rooming with Hank Betzina in the poorhouse.

So that was it, the old growing older. I returned to my cottage and resumed reading Yourcenar's *Hadrian's Memoirs,* and later, when my wife was home, an article on the cockroach in the newspaper. When the bomb falls, the one insect that will remain to multiply and cover the earth with its clicking noise will be the cockroach. There will be no boots, or man laced up in boots, to make them go away

FOUR

This Man (2)

IF I CLOSE MY EYES I SEE THE OCEAN AND MY FAMILY WALK-
ing slowly at its shore. A wheel of gulls spins noisily over the
incoming waves and on a heaped garbage can a lone gull
stands profiled, shifting its feet so that it turns to face us. My
younger brother races to scare the gull, but stops when it
doesn't leap skyward. He looks back at us. Wind is in his hair,
in his smile, in his eyes that are almost squinted shut. He races
back to us, a family on a weekend vacation to Pismo Beach,
this family that is surprised to be there with the sea and the
clouds and the sun almost breaking through.

I remember that weekend. My stepfather, home from work
and two hours of whiskeys and beers at Uncle Tom's Cabin,
sat drunkenly at the kitchen table babbling about how all he
wanted was to lie on sand and think about nothing. You can
leave me there, he said. Crushed beer cans piled up in front
of his folded arms. His eyes floated in alcohol. His jowls were
reddened into fleshy lamps. Just leave me there, he said all
night, beer after half-finished beer, until we climbed into bed
and tried to sleep.

Concrete. Kids. Warehouse work. He was a tired man when
he came into my life—two years after my father's death—and
even more tired when he spent days talking about the sea and
the whip of wind in his face. He sat in his chair whose arms
were slick from wear and oily forearms, the stench of vinegary
sweat worked into the fabric. He sat hurting from the endless
bend-and-pick-up of boxes he set on a conveyor belt. He
hurt from the house payments, the asking wife, the five hungry kids to clothe and offer someday to the world.

He sometimes dreamed aloud with the television on, with

a flash of too-much-drinking in his speech. While we did our homework in pajamas, we pretended to listen to his slurred echo of *leave me there, leave me there.* Later, in our bedroom we mimicked his dream, and bad mouthed his stench, his face, and his eyes that couldn't find the fork in his hand.

But his kids and wife worked into his dream. We all piled into our Rambler, drove the 150 miles from Fresno to Pismo Beach, and stayed at a run-down beachfront motel. We spent hours walking up and down the beach. Toward dusk we ate sandwiches in our room and watched the ocean fool around with small boats tied to the pier. Two times we went to an arcade where all seven of us watched others drop nickels and dimes into pinball machines, bowling games, and cranes that picked up plastic capsules of surprises. We were each given a quarter, which grew hot in our hands as we walked up and down looking for the best machine to play. I spent my first dime on bowling. The second dime went to racing a car. I wove in and out of traffic, sometimes slamming into the back end of other cars, and sometimes running red lights and riding up curbs to crash into buildings. I laughed at the mechanical flames but groaned when the game stopped suddenly. My sister and I pooled our nickels and played pinball while our brother Rick looked on . . . flipping his nickel into the air as he tried to break our concentration so that the final steel ball would roll quietly past our flippers.

An hour in the arcade, seven hours on the beach. We walked up and down, played tag with the waves, collected broken shells and rocks rich with color, and popped the slimy bulbs on the strings of kelp that littered the shore. Our mother and stepfather walked slowly behind, almost touching. They looked around, smoked cigarettes, and sometimes laughed when a wave licked their shoes wet.

Although it was a cold day, our stepfather did lie in the sand. He sent Rick back to the motel for a blanket. He shook it into the air but the wind tangled it. Rick and I helped him flatten the blanket and hold the corners down as he fixed himself onto it, face up. He closed his eyes, laced his fingers together on his chest, and told us to scram. Mother had already returned to the motel because of the cold. We watched him for a while but then ran up the beach to play keep-away with a soggy tennis ball. Later, my youngest brother and I sneaked back to watch him, our tired father, lie quiet as the dead. We crawled on our bellies until we were a few yards from him. He was very still, with grains of sand on his eyelids, wind flicking his hair out of place. This is what he wanted: to lie on sand, to quiet his mind and think nothing of the ocean, his kids, or the work that would end when he ended. I closed my eyes and heard the slap of waves on water. I heard a gull. My brother. My sister yelling for the ball. I opened my eyes to see a man get his wish: to lie on sand, to be nowhere but in his flesh.

Piedra

THE RIVER WAS GRAY-BLUE WHEN YOU SAT ON THE BANK, and gray when you stood on the bank, and swift and cold no matter how you looked at it in autumn. River rock splayed the water, so that it leaped white like fish; leaped up and fell back to join the gray-cold current, southward, to feed Avocado Lake.

Piedra. River of rock, place where our family went for a Saturday picnic. It was a fifteen-mile drive past plum and almond orchards, dairies, the town with its green sign, Minkler—Population 35, *Mexicanos* pruning orange trees on ladders, and our mother's talk that if our grades didn't improve we would be like *those* people. Past cows with grassy jaws, past fallen fences, groceries, tractors itching with rust, the Griffin ranch with its mowed pasture and white fence that proclaimed he was a gentleman farmer. We gawked at his ranch, and counted his cows, which seemed cleaner, better looking than the fly-specked ones we had passed earlier.

I dreamed about Griffin's daughters. I imagined that their hair was tied in ponytails and bounced crazily when they rode horses in knee-high grass near the river. They were the stuff of romance novels, sad and lonely girls who were in love with a stable boy, who was also sad and lonely but too poor for the father's liking, because he himself had once been poor but now was rich and liked to whip horses, cuss, and chase gasping foxes at daybreak.

My dreaming stopped when the road narrowed, gravel ticked under a fender, and we began our climb through the foot-hills. I was scared that our stepfather would forget to turn the wheel and we would roll slowly off the cliff into the brush and flint-sharp boulders. But he always remembered in time to turn and weave the car, its tires squalling through the hills that were covered with grass and oak trees. Then—just like that—around a bend the river came into view and our ears were filled with the roar of water.

Like so many other parents, ours didn't know what to do with themselves while we played. They would gaze at the river from our picnic table, drink coffee from thermoses, keep up one-word conversations, and smoke cigarettes. They looked tired. I felt sorry for them, but not sorry enough to keep them company. I joined my brother and sister in a game of hide-and-seek in the brush that ran along the river; played hide-and-seek until it turned into a game of army that would turn into a game of nothing at all. We would just sit in the brush and overturn rocks to see what they hid. They hid glittery sand and soggy leaves, smaller rocks, bottle caps, and toads and lizards that scared us so that we let out sharp screams when they ran along our fingers. We played games that we could have played at home, but it seemed so special to be there, the river loud at our side, the fishermen shushing us, dogs knee-deep in water and drinking.

When we were called back, it was for a lunch of hot dogs and barbecue chips and soda, and then back to playing. One time, however, I didn't join my brother and sister, but went on my own to hike toward a mountain that mother said would take a long time to climb. I told her I could do it in twenty minutes. She drank coffee from the thermos cup. She didn't seem to hear me. I started off, leaving my brother and sister to call me names because I didn't want to go with them to the dam to throw rocks.

The mountain seemed so close I could touch it. I walked *forever*, as a kid would say, and climbed a barbed-wire fence that said No Trespassing, and continued on until I was out of breath. I stopped, looked back and was surprised at how far I had come. The picnic table was far below, my parents just shadows on the benches. The river was thin as a wrist, and even Friant dam seemed smaller now that the gushing water spilled noiselessly from its opened valves. I liked where I was. The wind was in my hair, the sun in the yellow grass. I sat down, hugging my knees, and scanned the hills, which were brown and tree-specked and a purplish dark where the sun did not reach; scanned the road for the roadside grocery where we had stopped to buy sodas. Except for the wind it was quiet, and I was quiet too, with just one thought, and this thought was happiness. I was happy. All the badness in my life was momentarily gone, flooded with sunlight, and I believed I could lie down in the grass *forever*. I will have my chance.

Fire

THE FIRE IS NOW DEAD, THE COLOR OF AN OLD DICKENS tramp. Earlier it was red hot, sucking life from rain-green boards, egg cartons, wadded newspapers, and a log from a woodpile on the side of the house. I tossed the log in and listened to the snails, attached to its rough side, hiss their watery deaths. I watched the small teeth of flames eat until there was nothing left except embers that blinked and popped when wind swirled from the chimney.

I like fires. I like to light candles at birthday parties, light them not once but twice because there is something beautifully grotesque in candles melting down to their stubby ends. I like to set the dusty black coals on the barbecue, drench them with lighter fluid, and be the one to toss in a match: the fire bursts and my face shines like the crazed penny. If the chicken is oily, all the better. Its grease drips onto the coals and flames shoot up between the grill, like the hands of prisoners. I flick water on the flames; the coals hiss and steam and finally after hours in the dark, while we are inside and in bed, cool to gray dust under their larger cousins, the stars.

In San Francisco the bay is pleasant to watch, either from an apartment-building rooftop or close up. The sailboats dip and rise on the water; wind surfers skim over white-tipped waves which are pulled along by the wind and the moon's gravity toward the rocky beach. Children play in the sand, dogs frolic idiotically at the water's edge, and lovers fly kites or walk along, hip to hip, teasing the waves. But after a minute or so, the spectacle of the bay dulls to monotony: you look around and wish the hell you were elsewhere.

The picturesque bay is a tranquil moment, a house on fire

is a wicked occasion. It makes us stop, look up in inspired awe, become so mesmerized by the fire that an officer could tell you move back and you would not hear him. Your stare locks on the crumbling porch, a door wreathed in flames, or maybe the roof with its aura of hot sparks shooting skyward.

When I was a kid of four or five I tried to burn down our house, but (thank God) only managed to singe the back porch. This was my first disappointment in life, my inability to create excitement for the neighbor kids who egged me on to get the fire going. My mother singed me with a good beating, and chased my brother around the house with a heated fork.

Sometimes even now I will stop to stare at a leaf-fire in the gutter, just stare at the fiery tongues until my eyes water with smoke. More often than not, it's a kid who started that fire; started it but left because someone called him away, leaving me—and the kid inside my soul—to stare until an appointment calls me away.

Kids and fire. Christmas is around the corner. A book of matches would be as pleasing as a bright toy—and cheaper. But of course I could not offer such a gift, say to my daughter or nephew, "Merry Christmas, here's a box of wooden matches." We're not allowed to do this. But I would love to slip my nephew two or three matches and tell him to enjoy himself but not to get carried away. "Burn some leaves," I would suggest, "but leave my car alone."

Sometimes while driving I-5 in the Valley I will spot smoke on the horizon—control burning of the spent fields, a house on fire, a crazy with a Zippo lighter and a lot of cardboard? A genie of smoke climbs slowly skyward, and I can't help but think, what is the message? I've noticed that smoke doesn't go up randomly, but is circular, a clockwise motion, a thick-to-thin action, and high enough for all to see. Didn't Indians scan the horizon with one hand shading their brow? Didn't

Greek gods send down smoke and lightning to scare the hell out of man? Didn't the priest burn incense so that our eyes would fill with tears? Often I will try to *read* the smoke, take a stab at our fate, and come up with notions of wealth and contentment and long illustrious lives. My wife, who'll be reading her beauty magazine as I drive, will not even look up. She thinks I'm a little crazy. She'll say, "Yes, that's a possibility," and turn the page.

My fascination has nothing to do with pyromania. I am not an arsonist, or a person to jump up and down in delight when a hotel catches fire. Freud might write on his pad, "Sexual energy and the unconscious." He can write what he pleases, but I think of fire as an instinct toward destruction, which is both good and bad. Fire is savage, a reminder of evil which both repels and attracts us, and a hint of what is to come, provided that there is a hell for the wicked to leap through without rest.

So I have my little savagery. The fire is now dead, cold as a stone, but earlier it was hot as the first planetary flames. On this autumn day I sat with a coffee and stared and stared, and thought nothing in particular. I could have thought of lovers, a good fight with someone on the street, money and its finger-stink of evilness. But I just sat on the couch, transfixed by the flames that leapt and fell and leapt again. "Father," I could have said, "father, father"—for that is what it is. Prometheus gave us fire, warmth for the body and soul, and now clings to his rock, as we in turn give warmth to our children and in time will cling to our rock with no one to hear our small agonies.

Moving Around

WE'RE GOING TO MOVE AROUND UNTIL THINGS LOOK RIGHT, move left or right, into this house or that house, into a fancy car or no car at all. So it is with me and my wife, and now a daughter, a tiny reader who's jumping from picture book to picture book without so much as a word. And so it is with others who, like us, settle into one way of living only to get up and move into another.

If I look back I think of how we moved from car to car, most of which were no better than a faceful of smoke. My Buick Roadmaster limped up the streets like a hurt rhino; my $85 Rambler was ugly and died of ugliness on the way to the junk yard. My wife and I sold a perfectly good Volkswagen for a perfectly useless sportscar that gleamed in glossy photographs, beckoning us to be the happy couple leaning against it. It smoked badly, made noises, leaked puddles of oil in the driveway. The engine was so bad bicycles passed us up. Then there was another Volkswagen, then an Audi, then a Volkswagen convertible we still weep for that we traded for an Oldsmobile, which I gave to my in-laws after three years. I turned around and bought a 1966 Chevy that could pull your hair back, if not tears from your eyes, on a black stretch of highway.

We've moved from car to car, and house to house. Since we've been married—ten years—we've lived in twenty different places, two states, two countries, eight cities, and five counties. We itch to get up and go, to keep the body and mind moving, to find ourselves before a window that brings in more light, or less light, or no light at all. And once we're settled into a new place, we begin work: old wallpaper comes down, the kitchen is painted and fitted with curtains over the sink, and patches of earth are turned over for a vegetable garden that, after so many hours of labor, offers only a handful of carrots, some gritty radishes, and anemic tomatoes that bleed in our palms. We eat and feel good, but only for a while.

We look forward to less tangible changes, like new seasons. Today, it's April 12, the beginning of baseball season and breezy picnics, and already I want it to be midsummer, a 41-23 season for the Giants, and the sun bullying people to flap their shirts in front of air conditioners. I want, however foolishly, for time to hurry up with its shadows, to make things new so that my eyes can keep taking in a vital world. If it's fall, I want it to be winter, and once it's winter I want it to be spring, and once it's spring I want a sun and its bonnet of heat over my head.

It's the same with love. A few days ago while on my way to work, I was thinking that it was possible to start up with another: a young woman was at the corner with her bicycle waiting for the light to turn green. I was waiting, too. I didn't want to go when the light changed, but instead wanted to pull my car to the side of the street, park, and go off with her for coffee that would grow cold without us so much as touching it. I wanted to say something tender and begin a love I could later remember over a beer with friends. Yesterday, though, it was a different matter: a young woman on a bicycle crossed against a red light without looking, so that I had to brake and send my books sailing into the dash. I honked and said bad words under my breath. "Damn women," I muttered and raced my redneck car all the way to work.

Mercurial. Fickle. Capricious. I admit I'm all three, and maybe more. I don't know why I can't settle down and not move—literally. Perhaps I'm exercising my migrant genes: to break camp and hit the road for another field, grape, or beet. Perhaps there's a dissatisfaction I swallow like spit each morning but won't admit: my wife is my love, my daughter is my love, and all that hurts from childhood is healed over. Is there more than this? Is there more than family and family's good-hearted friends? To understand me, and people like me, it would take a doctor or a wise man with a beard so long that whole cities could hold on to it and be saved.

I keep moving up the street, looking for the new. And once I'm where I think I should be, I sometimes mourn for the days that have come and gone: the cars, the houses, the young wife who ran to meet me in a flaring dress. I look forward to what lies ahead, and feel a sorrow for what collects in memory. I'm in between tomorrow and yesterday, a Friday lunch date and Wednesday night when my wife and I played with each other's hair, kissed, and made a happy love that came out even.

Listening Up

IF YOU LISTEN UP, YOU MAY HEAR SOMETHING WORTH keeping, some scintillating phrase to turn over like a foreign coin and call your own.

One summer I heard our three-year-old daughter Mariko say, "The days are filled with air," and heard my writer self say, "That's mine. I said that." It was a busy Sunday at Tilden Park. Fathers were chasing balls. Kids were riding the backs of their mothers for gum, popcorn, snow cones, a hot quarter for a video game. Babies in strollers were drooling onto their hands, and dogs were prancing up and down grassy knolls in an utter happiness humans may never know. It was the kind of Sunday when a parent might want nothing more than to sit in bed with a newspaper as thick as a pillow, the blinds drawn, and the radio throwing out a tinny noise of violins. The day, and the day's shadows, would crawl by without you. The sun would look down over trees and fall so slowly westward that you would cheer the tagged-on hours you seemed to inherit by being alone.

But I wasn't in bed that day. I was among other families in Tilden Park, pulling my child here and there: the animal farm and the lake, the nature room and a tree-lined path that narrowed to a small river of leaves. Mariko kicked those leaves until she coughed and her eyes teared from the dust. I wiped her eyes and led her back to the car, and drove down the hill to the merry-go-round.

We stood in line, looked around, and then rushed to the growling lion, to the German music, to the spinning blur of people watching us go round and round with smiles big as hats—to her saying, "The days are filled with air."

When she said this, I leaned over her shoulder to ask her to say it once more. She looked up at me, hair lifting in the snappy breeze of the merry-go-round, and only smiled, not answering because she couldn't hear above the music. But I heard her: "The days are filled with air."

When the ride stopped, we got off and walked to an out-of-the-way knoll. I sat down with a grunt and opened our sack lunch. I couldn't stop looking at her as she worked her way through half a sandwich on her way to the cheese and avocado. Finally, I suggested that we talk about school and her friends or what she liked most of all in the whole world. She stared at me while chewing, swallowed, and rolled her tongue around in her mouth without answering. I coaxed her again, and she drank from her straw, cleared her throat, and finally said, "Your hair is a poodle, Daddy."

Little philosopher, sophist, wise-guy in a little girl's dress—she spoke a beautifully true line that suggests that the business of living (jobs, friends, love, failed love, and so on) is only air, and maybe not even blue air at that. All is transparent as air—a breeze here, a strong gust there, and people and days pass from our lives.

What magic from a watchful eye! I heard her make an observation that she herself was not fully aware of; it surfaced from one brain cell or another into her mouth and finally into my listening ear. This amazed me. We were spending a Sunday together. We were smiling in spring clothes like so many others when without warning she spoke a line of beauty, some truth to argue over all the way to the grave.

Probably other kids open their mouths to such turns of language—kids who themselves spin on merry-go-rounds with their half-asleep fathers holding the reins of wooden horses.

We're not listening or, if we are, we only smile and laugh at these cute spoken truths: perceptions that are more lush, more acute than the ones that issue from our mouths. They speak in clever ways, and we smile and touch their hair and let the words go, failing to remember what they say.

I took my daughter's line and made a poem from it. I gave this little one a hug. And an ice cream cone.

One Thing After Another

ON DAYS WHEN THE MIND WAKES UP IT'S POSSIBLE TO SEE that very little connects or can be reasoned out, like checkers or a quick hand of poker. Very little makes sense, especially in our lives. This seems curious. Last night, for instance, I was reading Montaigne, not in bunches, but in single paragraphs and sentences for he sometimes is a burden and goes on and on when he should be quiet. One idea leapt up in my mind and stayed there, like a blue flame.

We do not correct the man we hang; we correct others through him. I do the same. I relished the seemingly comic posture: Montaigne on a scaffold with his hair full of eager wind and some poor guy on his knees, a slack halo of rope descending over his bowed head. Then I read the idea as a bit of spoken wisdom and liked it even more: that through punishment of one guy we scare the hell out of other guys.

I read this master last night. This morning I got up and ran my index finger down the classified ads in search of a Pontiac Grand Prix, something with a tilt steering wheel and cruise control. I found a 1982 for $7,000, and drove to the suburban town of San Pablo where, at Accurate's body and fender, I sat tilting the wheel up and down. I adjusted the seat and the mirror that showed a piece of the sky. I checked the seats for tears or oily stains. A fender man in overalls came over and raised the hood. I pulled out the dip stick and plucked the belts and stared at the engine as if some oily part was going to do magic.

Okay, now how did I get from reading a great essayist to wanting to buy a car? What brain cell said, "Pontiac"? What brain cell said, "Let's read, Gary"? I'm not sure. And I'm not sure why later that afternoon after this business with the car, I spent a half an hour with a secretary talking about Puerto Rico and still later I hurried over to a luncheon honoring Paul S. Taylor, a Professor Emeritus at Berkeley, who is, in spite of his Anglican birth, the first Chicano historian, or so I would like to think of him. He's a remarkable man, and a sad one, for he is nearing ninety and is in ill health: his arms are thin, his skin blotched, his eyelids held open with Scotch tape. When he talks you have to tilt an ear in the direction of a weak voice. We felt for this man, our first Chicano scholar, when he said over and over that he was happy to be presented a plaque. Tired, halfsmiling, he held it up with two hands for us to see. The bronze plaque winked a flashing light and then went dark when he laid it in his lap.

From there I returned home troubled because it hurt to see a man in his failing years. When it is all over, is this who we become? A man with a plaque, with Scotch tape holding open the eyes to see just a little more of the world? I gave my wife a hug, called my daughter "knucklehead," and went outside to the garage-turned-study until dinner time.

After dinner I lay on the couch, belly full and groaning when my daughter, a play doctor, gave me a shot in the head and asked if I felt better. I said yes. She lined her brow, looking worried as a real doctor, and said there were tiny holes on my nose. She gave me a shot for every hole and two long ones for my nostrils.

I got up with a start before she finished my treatment when I remembered that the Mancini-Chacon fight was that night. If I can read Montaigne, mull over a car, and praise a great man all in less than 24 hours, then why not see the fight of the year? It was as good an entertainment as anything I could think of for the night. I called to Carolyn who was finishing the dishes to get dressed because we were going to see the fight.

A light came on in her eyes as she hurried to the bedroom to dress and remake her face for the evening. I drove our daughter to my sister's place—my sister, a fight fan from the year one, pounded a fist into her palm and wished Chacon all the luck. When I returned home Carolyn was sitting cross-legged on the couch in her thrift shop fur, waiting.

We drove to the Ivy Room in Albany, a bar with cable television. When we walked in the patrons on barstools looked up from their drinks to show us veined noses and eyes like red scribbling. They looked tired and heavy in their heavy coats. Biker types were playing shuffleboard, whooping it up when one knocked the other's puck over the edge. The bartender, with his shirt sleeves rolled up, dipped glasses into soapy water, shook them until he thought they were clean, and then immersed them in clear water. We took a seat near the television, which was on with the sound turned down, ordered a beer for myself and a Calistoga for Carolyn, and talked about our recently purchased house, money, family, and our daughter the would-be doctor, as we waited for the fight to start. We then went quiet, looking around. It was a strange place, this redneck bar. I snuggled my face into her neck and asked if she was having fun. She raised her eyebrows and said, "You sure know how to treat a girl to a swell time." She took a long and hard swig of her Calistoga as she looked at me with eyes big as they could get.

When the fight started, two heavy guys moved their beers and themselves closer to the television. One looked drunkenly at Carolyn as he passed and sat down with a grunt in his chair. He looked up in silence at the screen. "Ching chong," he then started in. "Let's get some ching chong food." He turned to his friend. "What do you say, Dickie babe?" His friend, whose eyes were on the television and the first round that had Chacon against the ropes, said, "What the hell are you talkin' about?"

"Ching Chong food."

His friend turned stiffly to him. "You're a crazy gook."

I was uneasy by their talk. Knowing Carolyn was Asian, they were being insulting and largely stupid. I tried to ignore them as it was the second round and Chacon was against the ropes again, gloves up and sliding away from Mancini's pit-bull tenacity. But the heavy guys continued with the made-up words of "Chow Wow Bow Wow" and "Ching Ga Ge Cho Cho." I'd had enough. I started with an Okie drawl with "Beans and weenies, taters to gobble up 'cause I got to pay for my fuckin Ford." Carolyn pinched my arms for me to shut up. And I did. Not because of them but because Chacon was in trouble. Mancini had him in the corner, sticking hard and deep into his face. Stay up, little man, I said to myself. Don't go down. But Mancini pumped hard and Chacon pumped back slowly as he slid along the ropes. Then it was over. Tony Perez, the referee, stepped between them to stop the fight.

I forgot the heavy guys and they forgot me because Chacon, *our* Mexican, our California kid, our baby-faced boy wonder, was on one knee and not getting up. We watched the replay of the third round: the overhand right, then the stiff left, then the right again. A leg buckled. Blood sprayed like glass from his face and his smile of the early rounds turned to a wince. We watched the replay again, then a third time, before I chugged my beer and led Carolyn to the door, thanking the bartender as we walked past the long, almost empty, bar counter. In the night air I was still troubled. How could he lose? He was on our side, I told Carolyn as we crossed the street against a red light. He couldn't lose. He was one of us.

We hurried across the street to Captain Video and, even though we didn't own a video recorder, scanned with other couples through the movie selections. It didn't make sense, our being there. But neither did Chacon's loss. He was our blood, a genius of the heart, and no way could he go down without getting up. We looked around for a while and then trotted back across the street for another drink to see if his loss made sense.

The Talking Heads

EACH OF US IS LESS A PERSON THAN WHEN WE STARTED OFF on our knees, and each of us has torn out parts of the heart and sold them for good lives, or bad lives, but sold them all the same. We lose that child of the heart by becoming adults who compromise their dreams for jobs, for grades, for small pay raises that may buy pants or skirts, shoes or feathery hats that cover up the shame.

One summer when I was out of work, I said to myself that work was for fools, and since there were enough of them in the world I was going to become something else—a reader of serious literature. So what was there to do? Drink water with my friend Leonard Adame and play backyard philosophers, sophists of the lawn chair and the bruised tomatoes. We conferred greatness on Garcia Márquez and Günter Grass, and handed out trophies to Neruda, Herbert, and Pavese. We pinned ribbons on Sherwood Anderson, Knut Hamsun, J.F. Powers, and Carlos Drummond de Andrade. Comeback player of the year: Nazim Hikmet. Inspirational leader: Miguel Hernández. Rookies of the year: Us! Adame and Soto, with 44 home runs each.

We talked politics, that foul fish for the cat, and made sense. We talked movies, Europe, and movies in Europe, until we were so excited by our talk that one night we bought beer and sat in the yard at dusk, when the heat of Fresno began to settle into the eighties and the evening light was a filthy pink, then a gray. That night we talked about educated Chicanos, those graduating from universities but falling for the "new car" and the "tract home on the Northside." The adults were playing "Disneyland for the kids, Reno for us." It was a simple game, like Rummy or checkers, and those who were intelligent, somewhat ambitious but not aggressive, and not terribly bad to look at could play it. For them, it was a thrill to flip open a check book at a fashionable clothing store and produce a driver's license and two credit cards. Though we talked and made some sense, we didn't say aloud that we were tired of this poor life and, if we had the chance, we too would grab the good jobs and go water skiing on the weekend.

Leonard adjusted his glasses and started with a flippant observation. "Soto, not even the dolphins are safe. Let one get out of the water and watch TV, and man he'd have himself a credit card in a minute. Beachballs for that guy."

We went on talking for an hour before I suggested that we have breakfast at the Eagle Cafe. I reported through the bedroom window to Carolyn who was sewing a new dress. "Okay, you drunks, but be careful," she said without looking up or breaking her rhythm at the sewing machine. I stepped back from the window and looked at Leonard with a drunken grin. "Yes, we must be careful. The waffles at the Eagle are deadly." The cafe was three difficult blocks away. A few beers tumbled my mind and ten or so weighted Leonard down like an anchor.

The Eagle Cafe was a sad place, frequented by used-car salesmen, mental patients, and old merchants in plaid jackets—those trotting through bad times. The cafe was a "greasy spoon" where, in fact, it was possible to slip on the greasy floor and get hurt. You had to walk cautiously—or wear baseball cleats.

We had breakfast and talked baseball, then football, then baseball again until we returned to serious talk—politics. But soon this grew tiresome. We returned to talking sports and then on to love affairs that were so convoluted that they were like novels we couldn't put down. But eventually we did put them down, pay, and start back to my apartment, poor friends of the same mind. We walked without talking, exhausted from the late hour and too many beers. In that moment, we were so close in our thinking that we were almost the same person, but only walking in two bodies in different places.

When we arrived at my apartment, we sat on the front steps and opened yet another beer. Crickets made noises in the bushes and in our heads. The porchlight threw a yellow glow that did very little in that dark of broken-down apartments. We sat looking straight ahead. We thought about how our lives could end here in this back apartment and how nothing would change. A dog crossed the street in our direction and barely looked at us as he passed in his search of toppled garbage cans and a good time. Leonard smiled, shaking his head. "More people know that damn dog than us." He sucked at his beer until there was only air, then threw the empty bottle at the hedge where the crickets had once again started up their machinery.

"Shut up there," he shouted, and the crickets quieted. The ringing in our heads kept on all that night and into the morning when we woke to a new day that was dressed in the same clothes.

Moses

I'M THINKING OF MY FRIEND'S COLLIE, MOSES, AND THE
evenings when a group of us guys sat in back yards to talk big
talk—women who refused us by leaving curt messages on
answering machines, and magazine editors, blind to our talent, who returned our poems, unread. Moses would join us
by sitting some distance away under the dead apricot tree, his
paws pressed sweetly together, his head poised and utterly dig-
nified. Of course, he didn't join our conversation; he was too
smart for that. We were full of nonsense about the opposite
sex, and full of beer, which made us stupid by the time the
night was over.

Chris, Jon, Omar, me. At dusk we barbecued chicken on
a hibachi. This was what we could afford, and tomatoes from
the garden, squash, brown rice left over from the time a girl-
friend moved out. It was a poor man's club, four guys and a
dog who snapped buttered bread when we flung it into the air;
a dog who nibbled at rinds of fat with better manners than any
of us; a dog who licked his lips, delicately, before he barked his
approval to Jon the cook. He barked, wagged his tail, and sat
watching us drink ourselves into a confessional mood that let
our deepest fears spill out, like mine, which is that we will not
be able to walk around when we die, and Jon's, which is that
we will walk around when we die.

But before we arrived at that drunken state, we talked, ate,
maybe played bocce ball under the grape arbor, maybe even
argued until we wanted to thump it out on the lawn. And just
what did we say about women? Well, for one, "What can we
do? You can't live with them and you can't live without them."
"Oops," one would say when a lover's period was two weeks

late. Being sensitive guys, we took sips of beer, reflected on the stars and the blinking lights of passing jets in the night sky, and peed horse splashes along the fence, being too tired or drunk or despicable to use the bathroom.

Moses was a civil being. If he could have talked, he would have told us about the female, told us, for instance, how to race for her without breathing hard, how to walk side by side without stepping on her toes, how to live with her without farting too crudely. When a female dog passed the house, Moses would get up, ears of corn, and trot over to sniff her nose to nose, nose to rump, and nibble and playfully growl under her collar.

He was a dog for us all. What child would not run a hand through his dusty fur and feel a warmth? What grandpa would not go to a knee and remember his youth? Even a mother, coming home with bags of groceries, would stop and go through her bags until she found the cookies. What man or woman, child or adult, could claim such love?

Moses was also better-looking than any of us. Orange fur, sad eyes of a French actor, snout like a party hat, nimble paws, nimble gait, up and down teeth that were white and seemingly unused. The four of us? Bald, or nearly bald, heavy and skinny-legged, saggy in the face and ugly in the mouth, even when it was closed. He was perfect in his fur, in his role as a dog, and we were imperfect in our flesh, in our role as humans, for we had only a splatter of gray intelligence inside the head. His role was to knock over garbage cans, look out the window, race to the kitchen when the refrigerator was opened, be petted by children, nose the skirts of our women friends, who would shriek and yell, "You nasty dog!" Somehow we could never understand our roles as men. Should we marry, stay married; kill or be killed; find jobs, or wait for the phone to ring and a voice to say on the other end, "Mr. Veinberg, we have lots of money for you." We were unsure what to do with our lives. We thought we should write for a living, but could never find that person who would give money for poems.

A few days after one of these back yard barbecues, Moses was hit by a car, returned home limping on three legs, and died breathing shallow sighs, his soft eyes blinking less and less until they stopped altogether. He went like my childhood dog, Blackie, with little fuss, with little noise about how he did no wrong in his years. His fur wavered in the breeze. He became heavy when we held him in our arms, this old dog with nothing in his bones.

The earth is richer because of Moses, buried not "gallantly with his feet straight up in the air," as a poet friend remarked, but buried lying on his side. It's a long blackness in the earth; we must find a comfortable position to wait it out.

Guess Work

A LITTLE WIND CAN RAKE THE SKY OF ITS YELLOWY BALM. It can do the same to the mind. In this autumn weather I think of the young woman I saw on campus today sitting on a grassy knoll with her gathered skirt pinched between her knees. She finished a sandwich and flipped pages of a notebook back and forth. A row of conjugated French verbs? Dates from American history? Math formulas that resemble eye charts? I wasn't certain. I watched her longingly, though, because there was beauty in her face and in her sophomore worry. Was it all necessary, her intense study for a pop quiz on plankton or the Dead Sea? Surely professors would not demand such stuff.

I know little about this woman. But there are clues. She was small, Japanese perhaps, and smartly dressed, which means she either had a summer job or is the only daughter from a good family, perhaps a 200—acre farmer from the San Joaquin Valley. I believe it's the latter. Her arms were dark. She probably helped in the packing house or handled a dusty Dodge truck that ran errands for her father, a gruff Nisei in khaki, who walked in his orchard that was weighed down with ripe apricots and Mexicans on unsteady ladders. I could have been one of them, a worker that is, but woke up in high school to see that I didn't want to stand on a ladder with buckets tied to my hip and babies screaming in my ear when I got home. I ain't gonna do field work, I thought, and went to college, sat on campus grass among other ambitious Mexicans, conjugated English verbs, read history, and worried over the up-and-down graphs in geology that showed the country falling into the sea, in 10,000 years.

But I'm here. This young woman is on my mind. Her dress was deep red, as I remember, and her shoes, the kind of pumps my wife wears, were off her feet and set like twin lamps in front of her. They were noticeably new, not yet scuffed or rain-warped or sagging. The fall semester was a week old. She had yet to walk places, say hello to new people, and, like so many other, take a boyfriend with whom she would pet heavily in a parked car. On Saturday mornings they would drink coffee and hold hands through football games. By the time their love ends, her shoes will be a clunk in the closet, and little else.

But who knows, maybe I'm wrong. Perhaps she's the daughter of a pharmacist, not a farmer, and she wasn't studying for history or biology but doing a crossword puzzle because she was bored with school. She doesn't like her classes, and thinks her professors are dolts and the campus men just boys who want to escort her to football games. She told one who kept reminding her he was pre-med that she didn't work as an "escort" and found football just dumber than checkers.

Maybe she's neither the daughter of a farmer nor a pharmacist but of a vice-president of a large bank in New York City, and she's a practicing Buddhist who lived her childhood in a Jewish neighborhood where everyone tipped his hat and was friendly. That's it. She's from New York, three time zones from home, which now explains her sadness to me, but doesn't explain the letter she received earlier in the week from home informing her the family dog died. That made her very sad, as did the B- on the mid-term in biology.

It's guess work. It's what I'm best at when the wind comes and the coin-bright sun rides above the immobile trees. It's a trade with absolutely no market. I can sit on a bench, clear-headed and curious about the world, and start a life without so much as getting up. Women come and go. Their skirts flare and bounce beautifully when they hurry to class or coffee or weekend affairs. They're young and hopeful. My hope is that the lines around my mouth don't deepen too much, now that I'm thirty-four and getting older. From a distance, when you look upon others who have no idea how awful it feels, anything is possible.

Night Sitting

I RECALL AN EVENING IN LATE SEPTEMBER WHEN THERE WAS no noise other than crickets, wind, and a dry rattle of leaves on a branch. My wife and I were huddled in our robes in the back yard that we had shoveled and watered into blossom all summer. Petunias brightened the back fence and the lantern-like flowers of the fuchsia showered petals in the slightest wind. We had enjoyed apples and apricots, pears and the neighbors' loquats that we picked when they weren't looking. The lawn, a triangle of green, had been cut a dozen times, maybe more; snails pulled from petals were flicked against the fence where they died a watery death in the sun. Less than two weeks ago it had been the usual cool Berkeley summer: low clouds over the hills in the morning and the sun breaking through in the afternoon.

Now it was the beginning of fall. In the dark of the back yard, our light was Carolyn's cigarette, a cap of red that outlined her face when she inhaled. For a while we talked about the day—bills, letter from her mother, letter from a friend in Europe—but eventually we gave ourselves over to the quiet. The stars were faint silvery points; the jets were steely lights cutting east and west. I thought about a friend, five states away, who was really much closer because I could imagine his belly laugh and the raise-and-chug of beer after beer. He's in Kentucky. The leaves must be falling where he is, great mounds you'd have to kick through to the car. Leaves and loneliness. Leaves in our middle years.

What Carolyn was thinking I don't know. She smoked quietly, shuddering occasionally from the chilly evening wind, and faced the neighbor's house where a young couple lives. And they *are* young. When I stop them to say hello, they seem unable to talk without holding hands. They lean into each other, hip against hip, and wave a bashful hello, then are gone up the street.

Love birds, I chuckle to myself, they'll get over it. But maybe they won't. I hope not. Perhaps love will hold up enough mirrors so that tenderness will see them through life. It should be that way. Let them hold hands, and be happy.

Carolyn looked in the direction of their house. The shaded window was yellow. Now and then a blot of shadows filled the window as one of them walked past, readying for bed. For us the quiet of the yard should have been a first step toward sleep, but my mind was awake as it recalled how my own heart raced like a mouse in its cage, banging to get out, when I first met Carolyn. I was college poor, a boy with nothing more than books and an old car. But still she said yes. Still she let me lie with her on the couch and let me make foolish promises that my brother and roommates pretended not to hear, even though I heard them laugh and close the door and laugh harder. Finally it had come, love and its spinning craziness. I held her hand and glowed an initial happiness that won't ever come back. That was thirteen years ago. Six cities. Two countries. Roomful of friends. A daughter with her own life.

Much has come and gone, love and those days when it was not love. How do we add them up? Who are we supposed to be after so many years? I know nothing about this, except that in a small way we are different from when we first started off. A line inches across her brow; the flesh gathers under her chin; a thin fountain of white hair is beginning where there was once a shiny black. We wake up to mirrors, fix ourselves as best we can, and go our own way during the day and come back in the evening. I'm always happy to see my wife. Her soul is a blue flame in my heart, not the jagged teeth of love-flames that sent us down a church aisle to stand before a Japanese minister who said things I couldn't make out. I watched his face, pinched with a seriousness that fascinated me, and wondered what his blessings were all about.

Last week we sat in the dark. Music was two or three houses away. A screen door slammed and a burly voice said, "Kitty, kitty, kitty." There was a sound of cat food rattling from a box. I got up and snuggled up to Carolyn because I was cold and imagined that she too was cold from the wind that had picked up, though neither of us wanted to go inside. She shuddered when I placed a cold hand against her belly. I brushed back her hair. I kissed her neck, rubbed my hand against her arm for warmth and nibbling my way down to her throat when I saw our cat Pip walking toward us from across the lawn. Sitting up, we both watched her approach and stop at our feet. "Pip," I said, "Pip, you ole'cat," petting her. I stopped my petting when I saw that her nose was twice its usual size. "What happened, baby?" I bent down to pick her up, but threw it away when I realized with a start that an *animal*, not our cat, was in my hands. I let out a clipped scream that was almost a laugh while Carolyn gripped my arm and asked, "What's wrong?" not certain what my fear was about. She bent down to take a closer look at Pip, and screamed, kicking her feet up onto the bench.

I laughed wildly and thought it strange that a possum (we had guessed from its slow crawl and spooky white fur like dirty pajamas) should show up in our yard. "Let's go inside, you first." I poked Carolyn to hurry up. She poked me back, hard, and said for me to be a man. We raced each other to the porch from where we looked back. We went inside and from our bedroom window listened to the possum clunk around in the yard and finally claw itself up the fence and disappear, leaving us still breathing hard but happy. We turned away from the window, undressed, and went to bed where we talked about our friend in Europe and pressed against each other. My hand, by then warm, asked her hip, "What do you want?" This, her hand said, and moved my arm across her shoulder. This for a long time.

Saying Things

WE CAN SAY THINGS BUT SOLVE NOTHING. IN A BACKYARD I can say to a friend that the rain forests in Brazil are being cut down, raked clean of their goods, and bulldozed into smoke and a smoldering ash. The Indians there are giving up. Several years ago a tribe, appalled by it all, walked deeper into the jungle, banged their children and babies against the same trees where cities would go in the twenty-first century, and with machetes cut bloody shadows across their necks. The tribe vanished, simple as dust. They didn't want anything to do with us. Their desire was to die as a people, not as broken Indians pushed around for a small wage.

A tribe disappears in Brazil, another in Guatemala, still another in Thailand where the forests are standing open like doors for those who want to make money. The government bulldozes, shoves Indians into graves, and trucks lumber that will be hammered and glued into coffee tables bound for New Jersey.

There is more to this: if the Indians survive, if the forests survive, they'll be less than what they once were. Bunches of trees are stuck together and called a park, a national treasure by the Secretary of the Interior who has nothing to do with the existence of trees but is more than happy to stand by them when the picture-taking begins. But in this forest roads snake though the trees, Coke bottles gleam in the grass, and graffiti of the worst kind—racial slurs, women with impossible breasts—is spray-painted on granite rocks, big as moving vans. Hot dog stands ring the forest, as if we need to eat before we sit under an umbrella of redwoods. Motels that look like log cabins stand at the gateway as if we need to sleep after looking at a bear buckle a trash can with his mighty paw. This is a park, we say to ourselves, to our children. We find it on maps—a shade of green, spread wide as a bruise—and we go.

Yesterday Pope Paul II gave mass to 40,000 Indians in Papua New Guinea. I noted a small number of these stone-age people, discovered only thirty years ago, was wearing T-shirts that said *I Love New York, Led Zeppelin,* or *I'm for Real*—or so I imagined on my TV. Most of the Indians were bright with flowers and pig grease, with necklaces of dog teeth, with feathers crowned on their spiky hair, raking the wind as they danced for His Holiness. But here and there, a T-shirt, an absurd pair of polyester pants on bodies that looked beautiful clothed with things picked from trees or shiny shells found on the ground. It's coming: in twenty years this tribe will run milky with disease and be flogged with debts for a patch of land that was once theirs just for living. Their children will ask, *What happened?* But it will be too late.

Nothing is solved. My friend and I can point to problems— cold sores in the mouth of the world. We can say this, and this, and this in his backyard, and not a goddamn life is going to change. We could, perhaps, get up and do something about the state of world affairs. We can march shoulder to shoulder with the anti-nuclear movement, with Greenpeace, with the Sierra Club, with the United Farm Workers of America's struggle to allow their people to eat more than platefuls of beans. In fact, we have done this. We have worked for such organizations and have done some good. Today we want an indirect life: we want to talk, to think about our fate, that blackness, that grave that will rain dirt on our faces and run a root through an ear until we can really hear.

This hand that speaks to a pencil, then a typewriter, can go on and on. I can say things that may solve a fingernail of pain—and isn't that a start? I can say what my friend and I talked about while we drank under a tree.

One, we should not eat more than two meals a day—the more there is for one person the less there is for another in a poor country.

Two, no income should be greater than another—a doctor should earn no more than, say, a janitor. Neither should earn enough to think he's permanent.

Three, all children should play until nightfall and read until they sleep.

Four, we should not wear more than is necessary.

Five, once a month we should walk until we become lost and must find a way back.

Six, curious minds should run the state.

This is what we talked about that night. Some of it is helpful. We would become better people if, for instance, once a month we drove to a place—city or countryside—and walked looking left, then right, as we took it all in. I've done this with a friend. We've walked through parts of Fresno we knew nothing about. We took in trees, rickety houses, new cars, people watering their lawns in the dusty twilight. I remember once on Pine Street we saw two kids, an Okie and a Mexican, taunting an old woman who was tottering up her porch steps. Maddened, we chased them until they gave up, cowering a little. We grabbed them by their filthy shirts, these poor kids with peach stains on their mouths, and yelled that we were going to bash their heads if we ever caught them doing that again to an old person. It scared them. They shivered like machinery before they said they were sorry and we let them go. They walked away, almost crying. We called them back and

gave each a quarter to buy ice cream. They were crying by
then, these kids that looked like us, only smaller. So this is
what we were like, I thought to myself. Little boys. Cruel kids.
We walked more miles to find others—and those old men with
hoes in their hands.

We can say things but solve nothing. Today I've listened to a
line in my head over and over: "the past seems horrible to me,
the present gray and desolate, and the future utterly
appalling." To me this bleak view is frightening. To another
it's a sentence not to worry about. We believe our minds are
singular and where we stand is the right place to be.

FIVE

The Childhood Worries, or
Why I Became a Writer

As a boy growing up in Fresno I knew that disease lurked just beneath the skin, that it was possible to wake in the morning unable to move your legs or arms or even your head, that stone on a pillow. Your eyeballs might still swim in their own liquids as they searched the ceiling, or beyond, toward heaven and whatever savage god did this to you. Frail and whimpering, you could lie in your rickety bed, You could hear the siren blast at the Sun-Maid Raisin plant, and answer that blast with your own chirp-like cry. But that was it for you, a boy now reduced to the dull activity of blinking. In the adjoining rooms, a chair scraped against the linoleum floor, the kitchen faucet ran over frozen chicken parts, the toilet flushed, the radio sputtered something in Spanish. But you were not involved. You lay useless in bed while your family prepared for the day.

Disease startled Uncle Johnnie first, a mole on his forearm having turned cancerous and bright as a red berry. He was living in Texas when he wrote my mother about his illness. We took him in in spring. He lived with us the last three months of his life, mostly lying ill on the couch, a space meant for my brother, Rick, and me. Before our uncle arrived, we jumped on that couch, me with a flea-like leap and my brother with the heavier bounce of a frog. Now he had the couch to himself, this uncle who was tender as a pony.

I didn't have much memory to go on. At age six, I didn't lie in bed at night, arms folded behind my head, and savor the time when I was four and a half, a sprout of orneriness. I was too busy in my young body to consider my trail of footprints, all wiped out at the end of the day. But I recall Uncle Johnnie and the apple pie he bought me at Charlie's Market. My greed for sweetness grinned from my sticky mouth, and we devoured the pie as we strolled home, I walking backwards and looking at the market. Later I would return to that market and let my hands settle like small crabs on two candy bars. They opened and closed around them as I decided whether to take them, thus steal, thus let my mouth lather itself with the creamy taste of chocolate. Charlie was probably looking at me, wagging his large Armenian head at my stupidity. But that wasn't the point: I was deciding for myself whether I should sin and then worry about this sin, the wings of my bony shoulder blades less holy.

I recall also when our television was broken and my father pulled the tube out and took it to a repair shop. The TV was eyeless, just sprouts of wires and a smothering scent of dust. While Uncle Johnnie lay on the couch, I climbed into the back of the television set and pretended to be someone funny, one of the Three Stooges, and then someone scary, like Rodan with his monstrous roar. My uncle watched me with a weary smile but no joy. I told him that I could be funny or scary, but in such a small space I couldn't play a horse or an Indian shot by the cavalry. He died that spring, all because of a cancerous mole, died after the tube was once again fitted into the television set. Then the couch returned to us.

For one summer in the late fifties, disease scared me. My whiskery neighbor, whose name I have forgotten, was a talker and addressed every growing plant, chicken, and dog in his dirt yard. When he got sick his talk increased, as if he needed to get out all the words that he had intended to use in his old age. He had to use them then or never. One afternoon he came into our yard and showed me his fingernails, yellow and hard. He held them out quivering, as if were going to do a hocus-pocus magic trick, and when he said it was cancer, I flinched. When I looked up into his face, pale as a fistful of straw, I saw that his eyes were large and bluish, his face already sinking in disease. I was eating grapes, feeding them into my mouth, and I didn't know what to do about his dying except to offer him some of my grapes. He laughed at this. He walked away, straight as any other man, and returned to his yard where he talked to himself and revved up a boat engine clamped to a barrel. A scarf of smoke unfurled from the engine, and the blackish water boiled. He didn't seem to be getting anywhere.

That summer we did our rough living on the street, and our dogs did too. When my Uncle Junior's collie got hit by a car on Van Ness Avenue, I watched my uncle, a teenager with a flattop haircut, gather his dog into his arms. He was the bravest person I knew, for he hugged to his chest what he loved best. A few of the kids from Braly Street milled around; the barber came out from his shop, snapped his sheet as if in surrender, and stared at the commotion for a moment, his eyes the color of twilight itself.

Uncle Junior yelled at us to get away, but I shadowed him for a while, barefoot and pagan. He walked up the alley that ran along our dusty-white house. I didn't know then that he intended to wait out the last breaths and then bury his dog. I didn't know that months later at the end of this same alley we were walking down, a car would roll, its wheels in the air, the man inside dead and his hat as flat as cardboard. I would be excited. Like my uncle's collie I panted, except from exhilaration, when the police asked if we knew the person. I pointed and said that he lived near the man with the motorboat engine and cancer.

This was the summer I began to worry about disease. My father was in road camp with my Uncle Shorty. They'd gotten drunk and stolen a car, but I was behaving. I drank my milk, ate my graham crackers, and dutifully picked slivers from my palm, but despite my hygiene, I was involved in disease. One morning my brother woke with his throat pinched with a clot that made it difficult for him to swallow. He opened his mouth in the backyard light and, along with my mother, I looked in, worried that I would have to wallow in the same bedroom and, in time, the same disease. His mouth was like any other mouth, wet with a push of milky air. But our mother knew better: the tonsils would have to come out. Mine would have to come out, too, no matter how many times I swallowed, cried, and said, "See, Mom, I'm okay." She figured that if you do one son you might as well do two.

That night I stood by the window in our bedroom and ate M&M candies and wondered about Father and Uncle Shorty. They were in a sort of prison camp, I knew. We had gone to see them, and Father had shown me his hands, which were speckled white with paint. I rode on his knee, a camel ride of excitement because I was chewing gum and sunflower seeds at the same. I asked him when he was coming home. Pretty soon, he answered. I didn't know that he and my uncle were painting rocks along rural Kearny Boulevard and hoisting railroad ties that became bumpers in the gravel parking lots of Kearny Park.

I thought about them as I ate my M&Ms and touched my throat when I swallowed the candy. Father wasn't there to help me. He was far away, it seemed, and I peered out of the window toward the junkyard with its silhouette of pipes, plumbing, and jagged sheet metal, the playground of my childhood. The summer wind picked up the metallic scent and whipped it about. When a sweep of headlights from the cars that turned from Van Ness onto Braly Street frisked the junkyard, the eyes of its German shepherd watchdog glowed orange and stared at me. I ate my candy, one last taste of sweetness on the eve of blood and gagging.

When we arrived at the community hospital, I hugged my pajamas and coloring book. I glanced nervously down the corridor. I looked at the old people's yellow fingernails, clear signs of cancer, and I peeked in a lab where I knew that blood was drawn. My brother and I walked on each side of our mother. We were led to a room where there was another child sitting up in a crib-like bed, mute as a teddy bear. He spit red into a bowl, and I immediately knew this was a scary place.

After we settled into our room, I worried not about dying, but the filthy act of baring my bottom on a bedpan. I was in a hospital gown, not my pajamas. I held out for hours, but when I couldn't stand it anymore, I told the nurse I had to use the bathroom. She wouldn't allow me to get up from bed. I started to cry, but she scolded me, and I knew better than to carry on because she had the instruments of pain. I told my brother not to laugh, but he was too scared to entertain the thought. I squatted on the bedpan and was letting my water flow when a blind, teenage girl walked past our open door, a ghost-like figure blowing down the corridor. A nurse was helping her along, step by hesitant step. I wanted to ask the nurse if she was blind forever, or would she one day peel off that bandage and smile at every bloodshot color in the precious world. I did my number and then looked over at the boy, now asleep and pale as an angel.

I don't recall my brother and me talking much while at the hospital. I lay in bed, touching the plastic wrist band with my typed name. I closed my eyes. I tried to shut out the image of the "thing" they would take out of my throat, a kidney-bean sac no longer needed. I knew that my baby teeth would eventually loosen and come out, possibly when I was biting into a peach or an apple, but I was terrified that someone behind a white mask would probe my mouth.

A few hours later, my brother was wheeled away with tears brimming in his eyes. If my big brother had dime-size tears in his eyes, then I, his little brother with just baby teeth, would have silver dollars rolling down my cheeks. I considered crying and sobbing as pitifully as I could manage, but who would listen? My mother was gone, a tiny egg of memory living inside my head. Now my brother was gone. I looked over to where the other boy was, but his parents had come and rescued him. I didn't have anything to do except thumb through my animal coloring book and imagine what crayons I would use on the deer, elephant, giraffe, and grinning hyena. This diversion helped. But then I was wheeled away.

This was the late fifties when almost every child's tonsils were routinely clipped from his throat. I remember the room where a nurse in a mask lowered a disc-like mask onto my nose and mouth. She lowered it three times and each time said, "Breathe in" as they basted my face with ether. I did what I was told until my consciousness receded like a wave, and I was in a room full of testing patterns, something like television when it was still too early for cartoons. They operated and later I bled into a bowl all night, it seemed, but happily drank 7-Up with no ice, a treat that didn't cost me anything except hoarse speech for three days.

When Rick and I got home, we were pampered with ice cream and 7-Up, a lovely blast of carbonation which singed my nostrils. I believed that we might continue to live our remaining childhood that way with mounds of ice cream, 7-Up, and cooing words from our mother. But too soon that stopped, and we were back to the usual plates of *frijoles* and tortillas. At that time, while my father and uncle were in jail, my mother worked at Redi-Spud, peeling potatoes that scurried down troughs of icy water. She would give us over to Mrs. Moreno, the mother of at least nine children and the jolliest woman in the western world. She laughed more than she spoke, and she spoke a lot. While in Mrs. Moreno's care, I became even more worried about disease because I knew roaches made a princely living in her cupboards.

Mrs. Moreno worked at a Chinese noodle factory and came

to get Rick and me after work. One day, when we climbed into the back seat of her station wagon, her son Danny was standing in a cardboard tub of noodles. His feet pumped up and down and emitted a sucking sound with each marching step. When I asked Mrs. Moreno about dinner, she was laughing because the baby on the front seat was crawling toward her breast. She giggled, "You like chow mein?" I slowly lowered my gaze to Danny's bare feet and felt sick. I had eaten a lot of things that had fallen on the ground, but nothing that had been kneaded between dirty toes.

They ate noodles right after we arrived, slurped them so that the ends wiggled like worms into their suctioning mouths. My brother and I ate grapes and drank water. Later, all of us—eleven kids—played our version of "The Old Woman Who Lived in a Shoe." We climbed onto the roof and jumped off, a cargo of unkillable kids hitting the ground like sacks of flour. It may not have been that same evening, but I recall three babies at the end of a long, dirty hallway and some of the kids, the older ones, trying to knock them over with a real bowling ball. There was squealing and crying, but it was mostly laughter that cut through the cloistered air of a dank hallway, laugher coming even from Mrs. Moreno when one of the babies went down.

One untroubled afternoon Larry, one of the older sons, showed me a toy rifle, the kind that you had to crack in half to cock and that shot arrows tipped with red suction caps. He took one suction cuff off, cocked the rifle, and shot the arrow into the flat spatula of his palm. "It doesn't hurt," he told me, and let me shoot the arrow repeatedly into my palm, the pressure of the arrow no more than a push. He recocked the rifle and fit the arrow into one of his nostrils. I automatically stepped back even though Larry was smiling. He was smiling just a moment before he pulled the trigger, before blood suddenly streamed from his nose and his eyes grew huge as two white moons and full of fright. He started crying and running around the house with the arrow in his nose, and I ran after him, almost crying. When his mother caught him by the arm, I raced out of the house, not wanting to get involved, and returned home, scared as I touched my own nose. I imagined the arrow in my own nose. I imagined blood spilling on the back porch. Later, just after I had finished dinner, I returned to Larry's house. He was at the table, with the threads of cotton balls hanging from his nostrils. The family was eating chow mein, piled like worms and wiggling down their throats.

The house was a poor, curled shoe, and it scared me because in its carelessness lurked disease and calamity. Neighbors came and went. I recall standing at their stove and asking a teenage boy who had drifted inside the house, "What's that you're making?" I looked at a large, dented kettle containing a grayish soup that he was stirring with a pencil. I peeked into the soup, sipped it with a large spoon, and saw small things wheeling in the water as he stirred them—a merry-go-round of meats, I thought. When he said, "Pigeons," I looked closely and could see the plucked birds bob and rise, and with each rise I could see the slits of their closed eyes.

The Moreno place, however, was not nearly as scary as the hospital. There were no instruments of pain, unless you counted the hive of tapeworms that showed up later because I ate raw bacon, white strips we peeled like Band-Aids from the wrapper. The Morenos taught me this too; they said it was good, and I ate my share while sitting on the roof, the sunset a stain the color of bright, bright medicine. How I would need that sun! How I would need a cure for my worry, and a cure for my brother, who was sporting on the bottom of his foot a sliver the size of a chopstick.

At age six disease scared me, but so did Grandpa, who lived just down the alley from our house on Braly Street. When I went over to eat lunch—yet another pile of *frijoles* wrapped in a diaper-size tortilla—he was at the kitchen table playing solitaire with a big chunk of his head missing. I backed out of the house, bristling with fear, because the only thing left was his face. He looked like the poker-face card in front of him: Jack of Bad Luck, or King of Almighty Mistakes. While I backed out of the screen door, Uncle Junior caught me from behind and nudged me into the kitchen. He told me that Grandpa was wearing a nylon stocking on his head, trying to grow his hair black. A stinky concoction of *yerba buena* and earthly fuels smothered his crown and temples. I sat down and ate my beans while watching Grandpa eat from his plate. I asked him if his head would grow back; he was chewing a huge amount of food like a camel. I thought I would turn seven by the time he cleared his throat and heard his answer, which was, "*Mi 'jo,* you got beans on your shirt. Shaddup."

Two kittens died from distemper and then Pete our canary was devoured by mama cat. A stray dog showed up outside our yard with sickly eyes. I touched my own eye, pulling at a tiny string of sleep. Everything seemed ill and ominous. Even our house began to slip on its foundation, which excited me because the bathroom was now at a slant. The water in the tub slouched from that one side which was higher. With a scoop of my hands, it was easy to force a tidal wave on the line of ants scurrying along the baseboard.

I looked around at family and friends who were hurt or dying, but I didn't know that a year later my father would die, his neck broken in an industrial accident. This would be in August, when we were settled in a new house the color of cement. He didn't live in that house more than a week, and then he was gone. The funeral didn't mean much to me. It was the scent of flowers and the wash of tears; it was a sympathetic squeeze of my shoulders and candies slipped into the pockets of my tweed coat, which was too small because it was

borrowed. After his burial I recall eating donuts at my grand-
parents' house. When a doctor was called because Grandma
was in hysterics, I didn't stop eating. I took what was rightly
mine and devoured it in the dark, near the ugly claw-like
crowns of a rose bush.

I didn't know what to think except that father was out of
prison and now in the earth forever. Because he wasn't
returning, I began to play with his squeaky hand drill, boring
into trees and fences. I liked the smell of the blond shavings
and liked to think that maybe father used the drill in prison.
He mostly painted rocks, this much I was told, but I fantasized
how he might have used it in prison to get away. I saw him
poking holes in a cement wall and then pushing over that wall
to get Uncle Shorty in the adjacent cell. Uncle Johnnie was
there, too, a ghost-like bundle of flesh on the cot. My father
was going to save not only the both of them, but in the end
himself as well.

Occasionally, we would visit my father's grave, where my
mother cried and set flowers, half-shadowing the oval photo
on his grave. What worried me was not his death, but the
gold-painted cannon on a hill that pointed at our Chevy
when we drove through the cement gates. The cannon scared
me because my vision of death was that when you died an angel
would pick you up, place your head in the cannon, and give
your neck a little twist. I was spooked by this cannon and
wanted to ask my mother about it, but she was too busy in her
sorrow for a straight answer. I kept quiet on the matter. I figured there was one cannon, like one God, and all graves
rolled on a hill. In time, you were asked to put your head in
the cannon and die as well.

I didn't realize that I was probably ill. Neither did I realize
how I used my time when my mother would send me off to
school. For weeks, I didn't go there. I stayed in an alley, kicking through garbage and boredom, and returned home only

after I assumed my classmates had finished with whatever the teacher had asked them to do. Sometimes I would take the drill and make holes, occasionally even into the lawn. But I had grown bored with this. I had discovered how I could make a huge noise. In the empty bedroom, the one my father and mother would have used, I spent hours with fistfuls of marbles. I bounced them off the baseboard, a ricocheting clatter that I imagined were soldiers getting their fill of death. The clatter of noise busied my mind with something like hate. If I had looked into a mirror, I would have seen this hate pleated on my forehead. If anyone, including my sister or brother, had smarted off to me, I had plans to get even. I would let them go to sleep and then blast them with marbles at close range as they inhaled on a simple dream.

My mother was alone, and in her loneliness she often piled us into our Chevy and drove us over to my *nina's* house on the west side of Fresno, a place that was so scary that even the blacks were a afraid. My *nina*—godmother—took in identical twin boys, same age as me but filthier. Their dirty hair was like the hair Woody Woodpecker wore. They were orphans. They were sadly nicknamed "Caca" and "Peepee," and for a while thy made me feel good because I knew they were poorer than me. "Peepee, is you dad dead?" I would ask. "Caca, what grade are you in?" I would inquire. They shrugged their shoulders a lot and ran when they saw my *nina,* a woman you dared not play with. Every time we visited, I took a toy to show them— plastic plane, steel car, sock of marbles, and even my brother's glow-in-the-dark statue of Jesus. I wanted them to know that even though my father was dead, I still owned things. After a few visits I didn't have anything left to share, just a ten-foot link of rubber bands. This lack made me mad, and I began to pick on them, even beat them up, in a kind of a Punch-and-Judy show in the dirt driveway. When we found out that the twins were scared of ghosts, my brother and Rachel, my *nina's* daughter, told them to sit and wait in the living room because their mother and father were going to pick them up. We gave them fistfuls of raisins. Rick and Rachel then ran outside, where they scraped a bamboo rake against the window. The twins looked at me, then the curtain that was dancing like ghosts from the blast of the window cooler. Their mouths stopped churning on those raisins and the gray light of the TV flashed briefly in their eyes. When I yelled, "*La llorona* is outside," they jumped and ran from the house, poor, terrified "Caca" and "Peepee" living up to their names that early evening.

I often attended church, a place that was scarier than the hospital or the Morenos' house or grandfather's head or even my new discovery, the medical dictionary with its feast of sores, blisters, ringworms, styes, and cancerous growths. Mother said that Jesus had been a good man, and he wanted peace and harmony in the hearts of all men. She said this while I looked at Jesus on his cross, poor Jesus who had nails and blood all over him. If they did that to someone who was so good, I wondered what they might do to me. You see, I was turning out bad. I was so angry from having to worry all the time that I had become violent, as when I stuck a broken shaft of bottle in my brother's leg for going swimming without me. Blood ran down my knuckles, and I ran away amazed that it was so calming to hurt someone who was bigger. My mother beat me with a hanger for my violence and then made me eat dinner in the bathroom. I put my bowl first on the hamper, then moved it to my knees, because I wanted a better view of the faucet dripping water. In the bathroom, then, I began to worry about our wasting water. I counted the drips to a hundred. I swallowed and pictured in my mind a pagan baby sucking a rock for moisture. Later, after I was allowed out of the bathroom, I took a pair of pliers and tried to tighten the faucet. I managed only to scratch the chrome plating on the handles, and I went to bed worrying that my mother would conclude that it was me. I closed my eyes and let the pagan baby swallow the rock.

I wanted to ask my mother if you ever had to stop worrying, or if you had to continue until you were old. I was already tired of having to learn about Jesus and the more important apostles. She answered yes and mumbled something about life not being easy. This was when I began to look at the pictures in the medical dictionary: ringworm, rickets, TB, tongues with canker sores, and elephantiasis. With elephantiasis, the scariest disease, your legs swelled fat as water balloons and, I suspected, sloshed some evil liquids. I looked down at my own legs, those reeds of bone and marrow. They were skinny, but still I worried that my legs could swell and the rest of me, arms mainly, would stay thin, possibly from rickets, which had made headway at school. I would be the second deformed kid on our street, the other being an older boy with one small arm that was shaped like a banana.

I knew the face of the boy in the iron lung. His hair was black and his eyes flat. He was motherless, for who could wrap a loving hug around a machine large as a barrel? I could hardly look at this boy. He might have shared my name, or my brother's name, or been related to the kid at school who had one leg shrunken from polio. I didn't like the idea of lying down for what might be forever. Still, I practiced what he lived by lying still on the couch until I fell asleep. When I woke I didn't know if I was at the new house or the old house, or if an angel had already picked me up and fitted my head in the gold-painted cannon.

Then I worried about air and radiation and religious equations like the Trinity and, finally, the march of communists against our country. The hollowness in my face concerned my mother. She studied me when I did my homework at the kitchen table. She suspected that I might have ringworm because there were pale splotches on my face. It was only dirt, though, a film of dirt that you could rub off with spit and a thumb. I was certain that communists, those silent spies, would show up and walk side by side with regular white people. In no time there would be too many to fight and then we would have not only English and Spanish but also Russian, a language that was like a record played backwards.

My worry lessened when I began to understand that nothing could really hurt me. It was another summer and the beginning of the sixties. On our new street, which was green with lawns and squeaky with new trikes, I discovered my invincibility while I was running with new friends, barefoot and with no shirt. I was particularly proud because I had hooked a screwdriver in a belt loop of my pants. I tripped and fell, and as I fell I worried for a moment, wondering if the screwdriver would drive its point into my belly. The fall was slow, like the build-up to my seven years, and the result would be either yes or no to my living.

The screwdriver kicked up sparks when it cut across the sidewalk. They were wonderful, these sparks that lasted no longer than a blink. Right then, with gravel pitted in my palm and my belly spanked by the fall, I rolled onto my back, cried, and knew that hurt and disease was way off, in another country, one that thanks to Jesus Almighty I would never think to visit.

The Effects of Knut Hamsun on a Fresno Boy

MY WRITING LIFE BEGAN WITH POETRY IN 1973, WHEN I was twenty-one and pinching nickels and dimes from an ashtray in the bedroom for my daily bread. But after reading Knut Hamsun's *Hunger*, I saw myself as a prose writer, one of those patient beings who fits sentences together and moves characters across a page. One summer, I started a short story titled "Ronnie and Joey," a tale of two short friends involved in breaking and entering, a common pastime in Fresno. I was twenty-four, thin as a broom, and with a broom-like head of shaggy black hair. I was newly married. My wife and I were living on Divisadero Street at Van Ness Avenue, and she was the one with a job—with the food stamps gone, our money depleted, our equally poor friends tiptoeing and clawing at their own empty cupboards, we had to do something. With my wife off at work, I opted to write a story. While I didn't see *The New Yorker* as its final resting place, I pictured a journal that might pay. I sat at my desk, which faced a small yard, and putting pen to lined paper, I wrote, "Ronnie and Joey were two piss ants living on the edge of poverty in a town where the worse you cried the more people laughed." I studied the beginning, the pen like a lollipop in my mouth. I decided to add more sadness and gave both characters teeth tight as piano keys. I looked out our bedroom window. A bird flew off a clothesline and, seconds later, another took his place, the line still vibrating from the first bird's departure. Surely this was a fit subject for a poem, but I was now into prose, a turncoat in search of a lucrative career.

I got up and went into the kitchen for a glass of water and leaned against the kitchen sink. I narrowed my gaze on a spider and then the spider's web hooked onto a stubby valve on the water heater. When I bent down for a closer look I saw that it was a black widow, the red on its belly like a fleck of paint. I nearly jumped when the spider sucked in its legs and then spat them out and got away before I could whack it with a newspaper. I felt a tingle after that brief encounter. Since I was inside the apartment and the shadows were still cool, I went outside in the hope of raising a sheen of sweat on my brow, a sweat that would oil my skin and relieve me of the tingle called fear. I admonished myself for being affected so by a spider, though I saw a poem there, too—something about death lurking near the pipes of the afterlife. No, it couldn't be just a plain old water heater but something symbolic and heralding danger.

The neighbors in the apartment complex—seven cottages owned by Mr. Ed Belinsky, an insurance salesman who was wealthy but often bedded in one of the small cottages. Our elderly neighbors, all inside, were either sick in bed or sitting in front of their televisions. Ziggy, a Confederate son and, from all appearances, the offspring of Old Man Time himself, was staring at his rose bush, scrawny as a rooster and just as mean with spur-like thorns. It was too early for him to totter on his gimpy legs toward the local bar called The Space, so he let his attention rest on his plants. I would have said, "Good morning," but it would have taken a long time for him to turn and bring up a smile to his blotched face and even longer for him to raise a hand in salute. Instead, I walked to the front of the apartment complex and assessed the cars as they waited at the red light. At the corner, they were wrapped in their own deadly exhaust—or so my vision had it. I made a mental note of this observation and then nearly jumped when I saw a guy I knew from school. He, a *vato loco* and glue sniffer, was crossing the street pushing a baby stroller. I remembered him from Washington Junior High because he had taunted me for carrying my books, he said, like a girl: the books were propped up in my arms, instead of swinging at my side. "You sissy," he sniped, then spit the shells of sunflower seeds at me. Since he was mean as a rodent, I had to look straight ahead and continue down the hallway, books still propped to my chest but slowly sliding to my side as I moved out of his view. That was in 1967, the year of peace and hippy love, and now, ten years later, he was pushing a stroller, a motherly act, with the fumes of baby crap blowing into his face. I thought of calling him a sissy, he with a stroller and a diaper bag swinging from the handle, but his knuckles were like skulls showing through his skin. As far as I knew, he was still a mean rodent, teeth slightly bucked and hair slicked back and, yes, a tattoo of a spider pulsating on his throat. Our eyes locked. He knew me from somewhere. He knew it could only be from junior high because he never saw the inside of a high school. He didn't say hello or flick up his head, as if to indicate, *"Qué pasa, ese!"* He passed, and I got to watch him push the stroller to the end of the block, wait for the light to turn green and—slyly—glance back. He knew me, but from where?

"See you later, mamacita," I said under my breath, but in my heart I thanked him because I knew he was a poem some time in the future.

I turned on my heels and considered Ziggy, who was still staring at the rose bush. I had a feeling that during my time away—eight minutes, ten at the most—he may have smacked his lips, a high energy activity, and pinched his crotch, "lips" and "crotch" being primary concerns for a drunkard. At three in the afternoon he would employ both these parts of his body after making his way to a barstool at The Space, where he would lift a beer to his face repeatedly until his bladder was full. Then, he would head to the men's room, where the stench could bring tears to the eyes of the heavyweight champion of the world. Ziggy was old and feeble-minded. He might have gone into the john and asked himself, "What am I doing here?" then pee his pants and respond, looking down, "Oh, yeah, that's right." Such was the fate of men who ruined their brains with cold grog on warm afternoons.

I returned to my writing desk and reread the start of my short story about Ronnie and Joey, pals because they were short and the world tall as Zulu spears. I had them sketch their plans for stealing from a rich person's house. I had the owner of the house dead from cutting his lawn: no, not the strenuous nature of the work itself, but from the owner's stingy resolve to save a few bucks. I had the owner swirling a gas can. With a shaky hand, he poured the gas into the tank of a lawn mower, which was overheated and viciously hot. The gas spilled on the manifold of the two-stroke engine and flames leaped up and lit the old man's shirt on fire. I wrote, "A carnation of fire grew into a bushel of devilish sparks," and pushed away from the desk to study the image. It was marvelous, I concluded, and then proceeded to drown the old man—on fire, he jumped into the kidney-shaped pool that was blue as a toilet wash. The old man flailed in the deep end, stirring up waves no moon could tug from the sea. Desperate, he spat out false teeth, which chattered as they descended to the bottom of the pool. He paddled to the edge of the pool, but his once-loyal Airedale nipped at his fingers and all was lost for the man who made his fortune selling gaudy furniture to poor Mexicans. He sank to the bottom of the pool, a snail-shaped hearing aid popping out of his left ear when his head struck the bottom. Shortly after, Ronnie and Joey slithered through an open window, unaware of the death and mayhem outside in the yard.

I laughed as I typed my handwritten scribble, the keys of my ancient typewriter nearly perforating the typing paper with their sledgehammer-like action. I got up and drank water and studied the space where the black widow once lingered, living on dust and the shell of human flesh, some of which was my

wife's and mine and some belonging to the previous occu-
pants, all of them dead now and grinning in their snug
coffins. Again, the poetry would not stop. I drank my water
and after such hard work writing prose, I went outside to once
again eye the cars, heat shimmering off the hoods. The fierce
sun was lowering the citizens of Fresno into one ass-kicking
headlock, squeezing out our bodily fluids. I made a mental
note about this poetic truth: we were poor souls caught in a
headlock of life by a bully who had the lordly high ground. I
returned to my cottage and fixed myself a sandwich, which I
ate on the couch, my fingers pinching, crab-like, for flakes of
potato chips. I drank water, filling up like a camel, and left the
house to walk down to the downtown library.

I passed The Space and then another bar called Mi Chante,
both of them nearly empty, though flies hypnotically stirred
the air. I came upon a dog with his tongue out. Of course, the
poetry took over. I had him walking on his claws, afraid to let
the pads of his paws hit the black fry pan of asphalt. The dog,
lost perhaps, was wearing a handkerchief around his neck, but
I told myself, "No, he's wearing an ascot." I told myself that
he was from a good home and was making his way back to his
master, but not before a jaunt through inner-city Fresno.
What stories the dog would be able to tell his offspring, who,
in time, would sport ascots and drink from clean bowls, not
the runoff of sprinklers flowing in the gutter.

The library was air-conditioned and the place was packed
with people sucking up the cool air for free. Most were children, or people like me, the jobless who would ghost through
the shelves and then finally sit down with a previously rifled
magazine. I fluttered the front of my shirt. Sweat washed over
my chest and its three hairs. My friend Michael Sierra, a poet,
worked there, driving the book mobile that stopped at play-
grounds and projects. When I asked for Michael at the front
desk, the clerk said that he was out making his rounds. So I sat

at a table with a globe that was large as a beach ball. I spun the globe and located California. I noticed that its surface was greasy and scratched, every child having tapped a dirty finger on Fresno, their hometown. I got up and drank cold water from the refrigerated water fountain and scanned the poetry section. They were all there, the famous and nearly famous— Robert Bly, James Wright, Adrienne Rich, Diane Wakowski, William Stafford, Theodore Roethke, etc. W.S. Merwin's *The Lice*, then my favorite poetry collection, was there. I picked it up and read a poem called "April," thin compared to other poems but worth studying because I could now argue against its meaning: if you lose nothing, then you learn nothing. I could argue that if a person keeps what is precious, then he or she could wake daily to its shadowy existence and learn something of its nature. But because I was a young man, the poem sounded wise. I closed the book of poems and set it back on the shelf, respectfully, because Merwin was Merwin and wasn't he so deep in poetic meaning that he had to be right?

I left the library and spied Michael parking the bookmobile, the air conditioning on top of the roof humming away as it cooled the shelves of books. I waited for him to park the vehicle, a muscular task of twisting the steering wheel back and forth because he wasn't given much space to nudge that whale into its berth. Finally, he cut the engine and he got out. I asked him, "Let me see the inside?" He let me take a peek into its dark cabin of books, the air still cool, and I was certain that this was the same bookmobile that used to swing around to Romain Playground, circa 1964. That summer I checked out armfuls of books and read them with my face full of apricots snagged from the alley. I told Michael that he had a good job and he sighed and didn't argue but told me was in a hurry to get out of the sun. I asked him, "Have you read *Hunger?*" and he laughed and remarked, "Nah, I've just lived it."

We both had to laugh. I left Michael in the shade and

started toward the downtown mall, skipping over a road embedded with bottle caps and glass, the archeology of poor people. Not far below the road's surface lay teeth and chicken bones—teeth of derelicts and chicken bones from people who ate on the run.

I encountered another dog, this lowly fellow not sporting a red handkerchief around his neck. But like the previous dog, this one was walking on his claws, fearful of the hot asphalt. His nose was black as tar and his throat surely teeming with fleas and ticks. I considered the dog and how God placed him in front of me. I looked at him and he at me, and through our chance meeting understood how each lived off the other's hope. I hoped that in time he would find a place to rest his weary bones before he died. And he had hope in me. I could see that he expected me to bend down and bring my cupped hands to his fuzzy face, bearing water or a half-eaten sandwich. He wanted evidence of human kindness. But what did I have but the salt of writing about Ronnie and Joey, still stick figures on three poorly typed pages. I didn't have much to offer, nothing but a sorrowful glance, and I admonished myself for not being prepared. I hurried away and entered the mall from Tulare Street, which was once a happening place but now full of boarded-up stores. And the few stores still open were poorly stocked and housed mannequins half-dressed, the clothes sold right off their plastic bodies. Music was piped in from speakers hanging at tree-level, but who was there to hear its violins? The birds, I was sure, had by now grown deaf from listening to the canned music.

The fountains were also making their own kind of music, spitting up spines of water, and a few shoppers were swinging their purchases in large bags. A breeze blew between the tall buildings, and the honking of cars echoed off the edifices. I whacked off a few more minutes of life by lowering my hand into the fountain. I wiggled my fingers and then worked them as if I were typing. I want to write a story, I told myself, but I'm thinking like a poet. I couldn't help myself. I imagined that my hand was paddling me into a better life, one with air conditioning and books so refrigerated that when you picked them up, they sent a herd of goose bumps up your arm to your shoulder. Then the hand was a fish, then a tamale dropped by a child into the fountain. I then remembered Knut Hamsun and how he had sat on a bench, touching the brass buttons of his shirt. Hungry, he intended to pawn them, but he was too noble to confront the broker, who would admonish him for being a fool. Instead, he drank water, the universal breakfast for the destitute, and staggered through the cobbled streets of Norway. His mind was dulled by hunger. It was dulled by the undeniable evidence that he was getting nowhere, and, in fact, was slowly disappearing as the pads of flesh melted off his hips. What was I but an offspring of Mr. Hamsun? I was another writer, a poet of many occupations, stirring the water for something good to happen. But since I was wearing a T-shirt, I had no buttons to pawn. If I fingered the inside of my pockets I would have pulled up lint or, perhaps, the teeth of a broken comb.

I yanked my hand out, feeling like a caught fish when I saw the rodent from Washington Junior High. He was pushing his *mocoso* baby in the stroller. I watched him pass under the awning of Lerner's Dress Shop. I began to think like this: truth comes and goes, sort of circulates like those flies at The Space, and eventually lands on what we think is good. Then, when the hand of God waves, we start to circulate again for fear of being struck down by the Almighty. I was doing the same, just moving about, just trying to find the comfort of shade where I could play out that dream of becoming a writer. But then the sun with all its sharp knives appeared and forced me to move.

I left the mall but not before swinging into Longs Drug

Store where Hilda, also a junior high classmate, worked the cash register. Penniless, I entered its air-conditioned environs and spied her—she was just lovely, no, better than lovely, a woman with a job. I considered greeting her, but she had customers with red shopping baskets. What would I say? And would she remember me? Me, the boy sitting in front of her in seventh-grade English and telling her that I bought my Levi's, by then faded at the thighs, for $5.45 and what did she think of that? I felt full of pride that day, but crippled many years later as I recalled my attempt at romance. I wish I could have erased that day. "Hilda," I said under my breath, and walked the aisle with shelves of plastic shoes and rubber thongs, Fresno Birkenstocks, as a friend called them. I held up a pair of rubber thongs and placed them back on the shelf. What was I doing with my free time?

I started my return to the apartment by walking up Van Ness, past a huge, grassy vacant lot, which, twenty years later, I would purchase for Arte Américas, a Mexican arts center. If a stranger had stopped me and said, "Boy, you're going to buy that piece of land and make us all proud," I would have thought that this prophet of the implausible future had fallen, hit his head on the sidewalk, and lay there until the sun boiled the noodles in his brains into soft pasta. But I walked past that vacant lot, well, not exactly a vacant lot then but holding out with a single business, a hairdresser. I stopped in front of its steamed window and looked in at two women with huge chrome dryers on their heads. I couldn't help the poetry; in my mind, the women were scorching *their* brains so they could forget their bad marriages and the jugheads they were forced to bed with. The women were lonely and whimpered privately in their cars or behind trees. Although they were heavy with belts of flesh around the middle, they were starved for love. I pressed my face to the window, then turned away when the hairdresser caught me ogling her customers.

The Space was now raucous with workers throwing back their first mugs of beer. Ziggy was seated at the bar, a draft beer set in front of him, and a pretzel around his thumb. It was a little after four. These men would all be dead in ten years, some sooner, and this bar would be gone as well, crumbled by a bulldozer operated by a man who drank there. Another truth: one destroys the place one loves.

I returned to my own place, now lit with the afternoon sun and so blinding that you couldn't look at it without scalding your eyes. I opened the door and a fly rushed to get out; the heat was overwhelming. I flicked on the cooler in the window, which threw out a breeze hot as jet exhaust. I drank water in the kitchen and then, on the second glass, fixed myself a cocktail of ice and tea with two scoops of sugar. I went into the bedroom, where I sat at my desk and drank my iced tea. I wished a pretzel could hang from my thumb. I wished for my own beer, even a flat one dead of bubbles. The breeze from the cooler stirred the few roughly typed pages of my story of Ronnie and Joey. They're coming alive, I thought. I'm making literature! I reached over and picked up Hamsun's *Hunger* and read the back: born in 1859 in Norway, he won the Nobel Prize for literature in 1920. The man was lucky: he got to live in a cold place and win a prize.

In a half-hour, after the cooler pads were moist and refreshing the air, our cottage would be tolerable. Until then, I decided to sit on the front porch and wait for my wife. I had news for her. I was going to tell her that I was through with poetry and that I was going to write a short story about small people whose desire was no more than a good meal and friendship, though first they had to rob a dead rich man's house. I was going to tell her that she was Ronnie and I was Joey, and both of us were going to walk arm-in-arm all our lives.

Getting It Done

THE END OF MY TEACHING CAREER BEGAN SUDDENLY WHEN, during a faculty meeting, the faces of my colleagues underwent a frightening metamorphosis. They began to resemble various chicken parts—breast, thighs, wings—muffled behind the sheen of Saran Wrap. Neither Dali nor Man Ray nor an experimental graduate student filmmaker could have envisioned such a moment—thirteen professors with the faces of chicken parts, their jaws moving and the words unraveling from their mouths like yarn. That was the beginning of the end for me, and two years later, after other surrealistic hot flashes and dark cloudlike drifts of depression, I quit teaching altogether. After my last class, I literally jogged off the Cal Berkeley campus, arms hugging bundles of teaching evaluations after thirteen years of rubbing my bottom on hard chairs. Happy that my books were selling, I took the beautifully redneck stance of "Take this job and shove it!"

By this time, my daughter was sixteen and growing into womanhood, and I, previously taut of flesh and bone, was putting on a ring of fat that baffled me. I marveled at the profusion as I peed at the toilet, my belly now in the way of my morning release of coffee. But here I was, heavy and not bright enough to put two and two together and attribute the problem to beer and the heavy sauces that smothered my dinners. I thought of myself when I quit teaching, and thought of my family—my wife and daughter—whom I had to provide for.

But I quit because our daughter was raised—or nearly raised—and she was now five foot even, a hundred and six shapely pounds, bright, kind and thoughtful, well read, and shy as a pony. I did my job of raising a child, and I'm not ashamed to call it a job because one of the largest fears throughout my adult life, perhaps instilled even earlier, was that I had to get this done, that done, that over there done, and even some of yours done if you were a lazy soul. I feared not completing whatever people wanted me to do. For sixteen years I felt that this daughter of ours must be raised, that I had to get her "done."

This was particularly urgent because my own father died when I was six, leaving a hole in my soul no bigger than a pin-prick. Through this hole something rare was let out, and I suffered because another person—my drunk father under a ladder—did not get his earthly task done. He had more of an effect on my character dead than alive.

I feared this mortal absence for my daughter, that is, that I would die by accident. I spent a good portion of my adult life thinking like this: that Mariko is now nine years old, almost ten, that it's seven years to adulthood and after that I can die and everything would then be okay.

This was surely not my reaction when she was born early morning July 21, 1978, born with her eyes open and seemingly astonished by her appearance, as if a magician had pulled her from a hat. She was flecked with blood but not much, and on a medical scale of ten to zero (zero being dead), she was a nine. She was healthy and ours, and quickly I agreed to a new title: father. I was twenty-five, and although still full of my own childhood, something that I slowly relinquished only after I lost the spring in my legs, I was ready for parenthood.

During Mariko's babyhood, I felt like a flower that had just broken open, full of color and light and maybe even a wonderful scent. Sure, our daughter cried at night, fussed over cereals, filled her diapers with monstrous debris, and demanded time and our money, even the quarters and grimy dimes piled in the ashtray. Sure, we read books about raising a child and monitored her monthly progress, worried that she was unable to roll over in her third month, sit up at six months, waddle bravely from couch to coffee table at eleven months. But her arms and legs were plump as water balloons, and she was growing. As we suspected, everything evened out. She would soon be in her high chair, then out of her high chair and in her proper place at an inherited family table, round and full of creaks and ancient ticks.

I remember her arrival into my life, and my own tenderness toward her—she and I rollicking on the bed, diapers crinkling underneath her pumpkin-colored pajamas. I remember her discovery of the word *pipes,* and her tiny hand clutching my thumb as she led me to the number of pipes in our house—pipes under the sink, behind the washer, in the back of the toilet. I remember when she let go of a balloon and we watched the balloon's flight over a flowering plum tree and beyond the neighbor's roof. She broke down, hands coming to her face and crying, "I'll never see that balloon again!"

And she didn't, of course, but she did see other things—piles and piles of food, clothes, toys, rides to the zoo and park, kiddie concerts, all before she was five years old. She was privileged, mostly privileged because of her mother, who was kinder than me, wiser, and sober in her evaluation of skinned knees and runny noses. My wife and she had a loving regimen—mother and daughter in bed with a book and, just before the lamp was turned off, a made-up singsong:

Sotooda Odooda, Podewda codewda, Ahooh Permew,
Peacock, Penguin, Pegasus, Unicorn, Butterfly,
Stubby, the best and only goat we know.

I had clues about what it was to be a man—to provide for family, to build something with one's hands. For a time we lived in a house nearly off its foundations, located on Cowper

Street in Berkeley, named after Cowper, the poet who wrote "Variety is the spice of life." I ignored that foolish axiom which only led people astray and into harmful behavior. I tried to put my house in order by whacking at weeds, rece-menting brick and stone, planting, silencing the neighbor's radio, and seeing the foundation, literally and figuratively, repaired and put back right. I was a no-nonsense Joe, full of vigor, maybe too much vigor because I became obsessed with getting things done. If I first took care of the house, I figured, then I would subsequently please my wife and daughter; I could then look forward to the more telling business of teaching and writing.

During my late twenties I slipped into a depression and I began to think like this: Now I will lie here and sleep and when I wake I will be better. I repeated this every night for three years, repeating to myself that I was asleep, while in truth my eyes were closed and rolling about behind the lids. I felt par-alyzed, listless. I prayed that, in time, the body would correct itself, like a hurt knee or a stab of pain near the lower back. Having been raised in a chorus of God Is Punishing You, I believed in waiting, expecting the gloom and confusion inside me to disappear like a scab. What was there to complain about? You had a family, a roof for this family, a job in which your hands only crab-step over typewriter keys. How dare you complain, my older, immigrant relatives might have scolded.

But the cement weight of insomnia left me slow of mind and body. I had a difficult time concentrating as I ghosted through my days, showing my teeth in theatrical attempts to appear jolly. I remember friends showing up at my house and not knowing their names, or what they were doing there. I had to leave rooms and be by myself for a moment, head lowered and a hand rubbing my forehead as I thought, Now who are these people? Are they my friends and Carolyn's? I remem-ber Wolfgang Binder, a German scholar, interviewing me while we still lived on Cowper Street. I felt tired even before he asked me a question. I kept thinking, This man is from Germany. Don't forget that. Germany. He's here because . . . and then the mind went empty as a pail.

Fear overwhelmed me as I realized that the possibility of happiness was beyond me. But I knew enough to try to appear chipper while our daughter was around, say, in my lap or strapped in her car seat. I mustered all my strength into one heave-ho, let's be happy, when our daughter woke, pink faced, in the morning. I had to live up to an image. I knew that fathers were responsible for taking their sons and daughters places. For us, father and daughter, it was a clean park on Cedar Avenue, or a jungle gym in fog-bound San Francisco. While our daughter played with spoon and pail, I sat on the edge of the sandbox, pouring hourglass after hourglass of sand through the funnels of my hands. It wasn't that I was bored, a feeling parents know because of their disconnection—nonparticipation, really—from their children's play. It's just a big, watery yawn watching children play for any length of time.

I anticipated this mental fog would soon lift, and clarity would shine through as if from an open window on a sunny day. I began to dread dusk and see it as a monster that traveled up the street, filling the gaps between the branches of the trees with an ominous symbol. I began to fear evenings, knowing that I would eat dinner, bathe, sit on the couch with a magazine or book, and then glance over to the bedroom, aware that I would have to go there and lie down in a veil of darkness. While our daughter padded about in her pajamas, still squealing, still making the most of her quickly disappearing babyhood, a dread overwhelmed me. Like a child, I didn't want to climb into bed and see the lamp turned off. The night was a monster that pushed itself into my eyes, and I was scared.

It was a dreadful routine. In bed, I convinced myself that I was asleep, though I could hear my breathing and calculate each restless turn. But mornings, my eyes were raw and, I suspect, punishing to look at from almost any distance, especially the distance my wife and I had created because she was living with my moodiness. Daily, over cereal and our daughter's laughter, I feigned happiness, smiling so big that the tops of gums were showing.

Knowing that I was ill, I was obsessed with seeing that my daughter was raised. My days were godless, uninspiring, a rained-on fire sputtering to keep a flame going. Fearing failure, I became cautious and tentative in movements that would risk an accident. I stayed home more and more, and canceled my subscription to the newspaper—why should I read about others falling apart? My hygiene became neurotic. Like a raccoon at a stream, I washed my hands before touching our daughter, say lifting her into or out of her high chair. I opened doors for her because the world was filled with germs that didn't show up in your system until it was too late. Eat public food at school functions? Out of the question. Invite a school chum to sleep over? You must be crazy.

During the height of my depression, I began to write furiously, albeit not brilliantly, and the subjects regarded our daughter. Three years old, she assembled a vocabulary that was inventive, even poetic. I listened to her quasi-philosophical turns of phrases, noting lines like, "The days are filled with air," a line that I later incorporated into a poem. And one day, while passing a chemical plant, she chirped, "The bad air has replaced the good air in my nostrils." When a Buddha-shaped poet friend spent the evening, the ever social Mariko offered him an animal cracker and asked where he was from. He scratched his belly, ho-hoed at her pleasant demeanor, and told her that he was from Fresno, the grape country. This was summer in our backyard. She raised her clear, unspoiled eyes to our plum tree and announced, "I'm from the plum country myself."

It's not uncommon for a writer's children to appear in
his or her stories or poems, to become the subjects of his
personal essays. Surely children rob writers of precious
time. They taketh away days and weeks, if not years, but they
also replenish our sterile waters. And it was true for me.
Through my depression, I convinced myself that if I wrote
about the best things in my life, namely my wife and daughter, I would get better. Ignorant and reluctant to see a doctor, I tried to write myself out of depression, to appear jolly
and a crack-up, though there were warnings in my poems,
as in "These Days":

In my dreams
A child is crying into a steering wheel
And Omar is holding onto a tree
And a shot horse is staring me into the next room.

That was last night, and the night before.
Today the two of us walked
In a park—cruel place
With pigeons bickering over spewed popcorn.
Later I heard on the radio—
A plane on the water,
And the gulls pecking the dead into great numbers.

Or so I imagined.
And so it might be because it's all possible—
The dead with wings in their hair,
Another war, the half-lid
Of the sun going down in dust

This scares me.
If we go up in ash we come down as ash.
And what are we then?

A dark crescent under a fingernail,
A smudge in the air?

Believe me daughter, I want to say something true,
That we will get up on time,
That I'll have coffee and you an egg,
Yellow sun on a plate.
But I can't ever say this.
The world is mad.
Dying things show up behind doors.
Soldiers toss severed feet for the TV audience.

Little one, stay where you are,
Hold hands, and don't let go.

I had an unfounded notion that if we went somewhere, especially on drives in the country, that these symptoms of psychic lethargies would dissipate like fog. I had to get out on weekends. So I pushed our daughter's stroller along pebbled paths, jarring her little frame. I pushed this stroller every-where, putting miles on her bones. We saw geysers, chilly beaches, small-town parades, country museums, cows and goats behind barbed wire, kites crisscrossing the sky, ponds with turd-colored frogs, and petting zoos—common pastimes for families with children. I felt that if I exhausted myself with the riches of the world, then I would sleep at the end of a day, happy for our daughter.

It occurs to me now that my attitude of Let's-get-it-done was also coming from the direction of our daughter, vague hints that said, Father, it is bad now but it will be better later. Perhaps her sweetness kept me from sinking into self-destruction. Perhaps the gloss of her beauty saved me. The more I wrote about her—poems and personal essays by the boatloads—the more the chances that this veil of depression would lift; the monstrous atmosphere inside my head would clear up. Only now do I attribute my release to my daughter, but back then, during this mentally confusing period on Cowper Street, I attributed this change to my study, which I had lined with sheets of cork to deaden the street and neighborhood sounds of kids and bikes. I had even placed a large, expensive sheet of Plexiglas over the front window, further deadening the natural and unnatural sounds of the world.

By fall 1983, I was getting better, taking less time to recognize people, becoming slightly more mentally focused. But was I there? No. I was still distracted by depression. I was working on my first prose efforts, recollections that would become *Living Up the Street.* I worked at my typewriter furiously because I was coming up for tenure, which, I felt, was another thing I had to get done. I needed more evidence than poetry and occasional book reviews; also, I was certain that if I kept writing, especially lighter stuff, I would heal myself. This was the real reason for my ferocity of pages and pages of prose and poetry—the effort to write myself out of a funk.

Nights. The house creaked and the plumbing inside the walls howled like the wind. Breathing in our daughter's room. I was living this notion: I'm going to go to bed and when I close my eyes I will sleep. Mind you, I did this with a peculiar pattern of sleeping on the left side of the mattress, legs slightly set apart, blankets up to my chin. The repetition was endless as waves, nearly four years without a sound sleep, convinced that it had to stop. Then the unexpected happened in November 1983. I woke up, groggy, heavy of limb, the corners of my eyes gripped by a squeeze of sludge, hair tousled and yawning, aware that I had slept more than my customary one or two hours. The wait was over, and I rose for my coffee, a different man.

I didn't tinker with my sleep by reading about depression. I was then, as now, not wholly curious about this illness, which can sink people to their knees, utterly destroy them. I would prefer to strangle all the self-help authors or honest-to-goodness psychiatrists than to open a book and discover what had happened. I would prefer to pretend that this episode of eaten-up years didn't occur. My business was a matter of seeing our daughter raised.

My father died when I was six, the rumors of his passing coming to me as I pulled flowers from a bush on the side of my grandmother's house. Interestingly, the day before my father died, a bird flew into our house on Braly Street, a symbol of death in many cultures. It occurred in our own household as well: I woke to a noise in the living room, a rattle that sounded like papers being stepped on. When I got up to see, a bird was in the living room looking at me with its liquid and soulless eyes. My heart leapt, literally, my upper body jumping of its own accord. This bird was showing me something, mocking me. I felt that it was after our daughter, then age six, the same age I was when my father died. With the front door open and my hands choking a threatening broom, I chased the bird from the house. I stood on the porch, breathing hard, the bird no longer within sight but somewhere hidden in the neighbor's tree. I returned to bed, shaken. I sat on the edge of the bed, then settled back in, only to hear the same fluttering noise. When I got up, the bird was again in the house, this time perched on wadded newspaper in the fireplace. Crazed, I chased the bird out of the house and would have pulled out its feathers, one by one, if it hadn't flown onto the roof and out of sight.

We raised our daughter, saw that she was loved by not only ourselves but by others. I buried her pets, drove her miles in every direction, bought her a horse, took her hundreds of places, and saw, above all, to get her an education. Moreover, during my time with her, I feigned happiness when, in truth, my depression was as insurmountable as the Himalayas.

Wasn't this something? I gave her life and she returned it to me by her presence.

Occasionally I see fathers with their daughters, fathers who, on first glance, might be bored as they hover over them at play. But how many are ill, mentally pulled into themselves, depressed and fraudulent protectors, bad clowns squeezing out their own cajoling laughter? On the surface, these fathers may appear familial magistrates for their children, fathers who loom tall as trees. They are cheerful; they hold pails for them, toys, or upright spilled trikes. They carefully peel back ice cream wrappers and rub a healthy gloss on apples. They are young fathers, not unlike me sixteen years before. What's in the heart? I sometimes wonder. What advice could I, a man walking past, offer? How could I solve the first crisis of a child falling over shoelaces? Or the serious struggles that follow? I walk past, or jog past. What can I say in my injured heart? My friend, the world was ill, and still I got it done.

Who Is Your Reader?

MY FIRST BOOK OF POEMS, *THE ELEMENTS OF SAN JOAQUIN*, WAS published in spring 1977 and dedicated in part to *mi abuelita*. My grandmother fled Mexico in 1914, somewhere in the middle of the Mexican Revolution, and like many other early immigrants, legal and otherwise, could read neither Spanish nor English; her grasp of the world was purely verbal or dependent upon pictures. As a young man of twenty-five, I did my filial duty by giving her a copy of my book. Grandma's reaction was to smile at its dull, university-press-designed book jacket, and bunch her brow into creases deep enough to sow seeds; she realized an occasion was upon her and fixed me a glorious meal on her four-burner stove—eggs, *frijoles*, and tortillas. I don't remember what came first, the meal or her hunt for a picture frame into which she fit my book. She placed it on a coffee table in her living room that was entirely decorated in red—sofa, curtains, carpet, and cute ceramic sculptures. In that museum of bad taste, my book was the centerpiece.

Would Grandma be typical of my readership? Would others smile at my book, pat my shoulder for my effort to promote Chicano literacy and literature, and then put it in a picture frame? Undaunted, I pedaled my bike through Fresno to deliver copies of my book to other friends and relatives as evidence that I was on the right track.

From all appearances, my days in the grape and cotton fields were a thing of the past. The year was 1977, and I was aware that my poetry would likely be read by only a select few outside of Chicano Studies classes. By then, my wife and I were living at the corner of Van Ness and Divisadero in downtown

Fresno, where at night everyone, winos included, cleared out, leaving behind a few cats to piss, fight, copulate, and Dumpster-hop their way toward beastly ecstasy. The place could be spooky, especially in the red glow of the porno theater, the Venus, whose lights winked and beckoned me, though I crossed the street but once to enter that moist cavern.

A merchant at heart, I held a book party at our little downtown cottage. My wife may or my not have cut squares of cheese and such, the "such" being the ubiquitous cauliflower buds and carrot sticks that are the fodder of every English Department gathering. I sold a few books that afternoon; thus I was happy, if not slightly drunk on my own success, and assumed that I was on my way. The party even gave me confidence: I took my bike down to *The Fresno Bee*, where Eddie Lopez, a features writer, wrote a short article on me—"From former farmworker to Noted Chicano Poet," the caption read. A picture was taken of me; I looked all of fourteen years old, with a rabbit-ear cowlick projecting from the back of my head. Friends were amazed that I had made the inside of the newspaper without being trouble!

How do you get people to read your work, I wondered. Aside from a few Fresno poets, my acquaintances could only point at the pictures in a Denny's menu—the Grand Slam having more value than my poems about death and field work. This has always been a problem with poets, that is, how to get their book into another person's hands. For me the problem was especially acute since my prospective reader was brown and callused from labor. I turned this question over and let it go because the task was monumental. Why bother, I thought. I only had one single collection slim enough to fit in a picture frame.

That summer, when both Elvis and Robert Lowell died (this memory won't wash away), I wrote poetry *and* fiction, the margin-to-margin prose a villainous temptation for rustling up a larger readership. The characters of my first short story, titled "Ronnie and Joey Get Their Way," violated every tenet of political correctness, so I won't bother to construct (or deconstruct) the narrative, written with glee on my Royal typewriter. But I did offer to read this piece in public in 1978 at the Reno Club in Sacramento. José Montoya and his cohorts in the Royal Chicano Airforce held a read-in at the bar, where the year before a fist fight erupted between two Chicano factions. The argument, I gathered from hearsay, involved who was the best, most authentic, *el mero chingón,* Chicano poet of Aztlán. The question could only be solved in the parking lot, thought that bunch of gold-toothed pirates.

I read my short story and the crowd yukked it up because the story was light yet filthy, and tender because the poor people were going to win. I knew my rough-and-ready audience with puddles of beer on their wobbly tables and drunken faces loose as sacks. That night I could have chucked my poetry and turned to commercial prose and become another Bukowski, Crumley, Harry Crews, or the stylish but comical Thomas Berger, master of them all.

But no such luck. I cowered under the threat of living on Top Ramen at the corner of Van Ness and Divisadero, cowered because I was twenty-five and acutely aware that I should get on with a profession. In short, I searched for a teaching job and, in time, became an assistant professor of Chicano Studies and English, fathered a child, assumed a mortgage, etc. For ten years I continued writing and publishing poetry before I reread my story about Ronnie and Joey, two little scoundrels who robbed Fresno blind. The story brought a huge grin to my face. I felt giddy, optimistic. I put aside poetry and quickly wrote a book-length memoir of growing up Mexican American in Fresno during the 1950s and 60s. This became *Living Up the Street,* composed in longhand at our dining table and, I see now, through a depression as large and ugly as Godzilla. Published in 1985 by a small commercial house and subsequently a large press, it became what could be described as an underground classic.

Despite my momentary retreat from poetry, I remained a poet and not above moving my books so they faced *outwards* at a bookstore in order to catch the eye of a potential book buyer. Such ambition! Such youth, really. Moreover, I still believed in poetry readings, mine and others. I recall being paired up to read with poet George Evans at San Francisco's Intersection. There were four or five lonely souls in the audience and, assigned to read first, I asked each one of them, "Why are you here?" I may have asked with a droopy-eyed sadness on my face. Ah, come on, tell me you're here because of me, I nearly begged. Each of them said thoughtlessly: "I'm here because of George."

Readership. The agony of writing is a terror in itself, but to build an audience once a book is published? I'm leaving out much between my poetry years of 1981 to 1989, years in which a whole herd of other Chicano poets would love to have tarred and feathered me if the law allowed, years in which only a few book reviews and no criticism was written on my poetry, not an uncommon experience among contemporary poets, I admit. I leave out so much detail to arrive at a place my fellow poets may imagine impossible. It even strikes me as inconceivable, but between spring 1990 and spring 1998 my work for children, young adults, and adults has sold over a million copies; on average, the books sell seven thousand copies a month. I mention these figures out of astonishment, not the desire to gloat. Something is happening, and most other writers and scholars, aren't aware of a commercial shift to my corner where also sit Sandra Cisneros, Rudy Anaya, Denise Chavez, and Ana Castillo, *los meros, meros.* Moreover, I'm alerting the reader that I don't teach, having taken to heart that country-western favorite,

"Take this Job, and Shove it." I left that profession of headaches several years ago because of grade-grubbing students and my insulting salary—after twelve years of chalk dust, my half-time salary at Cal Berkeley was $28,800. I don't hobnob, do poetry readings or summer workshops, win literary awards, sit on panels, give interviews, offer blurbs, appear in *Poets and Writers,* and except for the Kingsley Tufts Award don't judge contests; my literary life doesn't follow convention and these brief remarks are about that: how one poet built up a readership despite the comments of people like Harold Bloom, who stated in *Newsweek,* "Gary Soto couldn't write himself out of a paper bag." A livid and knee-jerk response to work he probably hasn't read? I cringe when I imagine what comments come out of the old prof's mouth when he's not on duty.

I can dismiss such scolding scholars. However, I can't dismiss the reactions to my work in elementary, middle grade, high schools, and colleges throughout California. This poet has gassed up his car and gone forth to meet his readers. Over a nine-year period I have spoken to three hundred thousand teachers and students, possibly more, and was—this gets stranger—an NBC News Friday-night focus of the week, a feature that was subsequently run on continental United Airlines flights. In my garage sit boxes of fan letters and hand-drawn banners proclaiming me the best writer in the world. (If the kids really knew!) And why such a reception? Unlike most other contemporary poets and writers, I've taken the show on the road and built a name among *la gente,* the people. I have ventured into schools where I have played baseball and basketball with young people, sung songs, acted in skits, delivered commencement speeches, learned three chords on a Mexican guitar to serenade teachers, formed a touring *teatro,* saw that my opera *Nerdlandia* was mounted in high schools, established scholarships, and given away thousands of dollars to Chicano cultural centers. I have gone to prisons and mingled with people who have done time. (Once, when I was making a super-eight movie in East Los Angeles, a true gang banger insisted on directing a scene. Since he was built like G.I. Joe and one click of his fingers made other *vatos* stop in their tracks, I decided it would be in the best interest of my health, if not my art, to let him cry, "Action.") Almost every Chicano youth and teacher is familiar with my name. I was even approached by someone who wanted to name a building after me. When I inquired of its purpose, she said, "a teen pregnancy center." I begged them to remove my name from consideration.

My readership is strung from large cities, such as Los Angeles, to dinky Del Rey where peach trees outnumber the population by many thousands. From all appearances, my readers care. Once, I was given a parade in Huron, California. The town, nearly all Mexican or Mexican American, numbered four thousand that winter when the mayor proclaimed Gary Soto Day. Because the town was small—three commercial blocks long—we had to start the parade of eight hundred celebrants in the grape vineyards, the spinning red lights of a fire engine pulsating on our faces. I sat in the back of a Chevy convertible while waving to the Spanish-speaking crowd as they came out of bars, a laundromat, the three Mexican restaurants, and the local Foster Freeze. Sure, I felt silly, but it had to be done. The crowds watched as we made our way toward the school. There, I premiered my little 16mm film, "The Bike," which featured the good people from Huron as the principal actors. Why go to the San Francisco Film Festival when a school cafeteria will do? I showed the film on a clean wall but not before a bike was auctioned off and my Uncle Shorty, one of the actors, was assigned the duty of judging the Gary Soto portraits done by first graders. I was portrayed with a square head, big ears, spooked eyes—all the body parts of a happy-go-lucky Frankenstein.

Are these my readers? Is this my fame, my earthly reward played out in the grape fields I had wanted so much to escape? That night I had to stack the chairs and later pay for dinner— treating sixteen kids at a Mexican restaurant was an unwise move on my part! Of course, when I speak to college students I put on another face, one that is nearly serene and erudite. But these are rare moments as my appearances grow more and more casual. I think of last week when I led a school parade, again in my honor, at Winchell Elementary in Fresno, a school I attended for two brief months in the fall of 1959. (Winchell, I suspect, claims me as its own, though Jefferson Elementary is willing to fight for me because I was a full-fledged student there for two years.) That day there were skits and songs, chicken *mole* and hand-made tortillas, and a little dramatic skit between me and David Ricardo, the school's vice-principal and a former high school wrestler who once tore me to pieces. The day was even more touching because my high school wrestling coach, Mr. DeCarlo, made an appearance and told everyone, "Oh, Gary was a good wrestler." Hey, what's a little lie between old friends?

The following day I addressed fifteen hundred teachers for the Fresno Unified School District; the theme was "Cultivating Excellence," which portended a serious tone and for which they expected me to sound like Dr. Martin Luther King, Jr. Since there was talk of the teachers going on strike, I knew my act that morning. I shuffled my notes, looked up and down several times, and then crowed to the teachers, "If we're going to cultivate excellence, don't we need excellent salaries?" They screamed and applauded as if I had made a touchdown. I didn't bother to grin at the chief administrators of the school district or two school board members seated in the front row. Other than cross and recross their legs, they couldn't contradict me with all those teachers on my team.

That afternoon I flew to Orange County where I made an appearance at Los Amigos High School in Fountain Valley. Earlier in the year, four students acted scenes from my one-act play *Novio Boy*. These young, first-time actors were brilliant as they performed first at Martinez's Bookstore in Santa Ana and then for the faculty at their high school. I loved those kids and was so high on their exuberance that I later escorted them (with the drama teacher, Leigh Nicolls, in tow) to a mall and bought each of them a pair of shoes—I felt more than a little awkward as the young women, twelfth-graders, slipped into sandals, and one of them asked, "What do you think, Mr. Soto?" *Ay, por favor, muchacha,* I thought. Have mercy on this old man!

When the full-fledged play was performed a few months later at Los Amigos High School, I showed up to see my play, mingle and shake hands, and be a famous figure, seeing that famous figures were difficult to come by. In short, I signed programs and books from the vendor Cafe con Libros, and sat in the dark to watch the comedy play itself out to laughter and applause. The principal actors—Diego, Janet, Karina, and Alex—were lovely to watch. But where was the true entertainment? On stage *or* in the audience where I sat laughing and stomping my feet at my own low-class Chicano humor. Afterwards, I fielded two questions and we ended the evening with a United Farm Workers handclap, one that starts slowly and builds toward a crescendo of a palm-stinging appreciation. Then we were off to Roundtable Pizza and, once again, I was feeding teenagers, those piranhas that are all teeth and hollow legs.

There was no one to document that evening, or what I've been up to these last nine years, in part because there are so few Chicano scholars. That night after my play, I and my host Alejandro Morales, UC Irvine Spanish professor and novelist, counted the number of Chicanos teaching literature in the UC system. Not counting those in Ethnic Studies departments, we knew of only a handful: five in English departments, that is, five out of 410 tenure-track positions. Alejandro figured that there were an equal number in Spanish departments statewide, and perhaps a couple in the field of comparative literature. We figured that in literature and creative writing programs and departments as a whole there were only thirteen tenure-track professors, thirteen out of 670 positions in a state where there are nine million Latinos. If I had had a guitar, I would have let out a *grito* and strummed the three chords of grief; instead, I did the next best thing: I drank more of Alejandro's excellent wine. Then I recalled another evening spent with Professor Hector Torres from the University of New Mexico. We, too, counted the number of Chicanos in English departments nationwide, summing up forty-one such professors who held tenure-track positions, forty-one from God-knows-how-many thousands of positions. You need more than wine to overcome these dismal figures. So much for affirmative action, and so much for the documentation of my work or the work of other Chicanos who are creating literary history.

But finally, teaching is someone else's business. My business is to make readers from non-readers, and if you think it's easy—or self-serving because my books are being bought—then join me anytime and see how, where, and why it's done. On the "where" front, I have slept on a lot of floors and couches, and on the "why" front I recall the kinder, gentler America that was proposed several years ago. And where is that America? Because I believe in literature and the depth of living it adds to our years, my task is to start Chicanos reading. If it's my poetry, great. If it's Sandra Cisneros's prose, that's great as well. If Chicanos start with other writers, say Hemingway or Kaye Gibbons or the stately prose of Anita Brookner, that's fine too. As for me, I start with kindergarteners, most of whom are Spanish-speaking and weigh in at forty-five pounds, and move up to the college students, not to mention those *abuelitas* who are curious to see how I turned out after all the stupid antics I portrayed in *Living Up the Street.* I'm in their lives and in their hearts. I'm searching for a family whose grandmother, an illiterate, fits a book into a picture frame, the centerpiece for a household that will in time quiet down and throw open the cover.

Acknowledgments

The present volume includes all of the work previously collected in *Small Faces* (1986): "The Jacket," "The Arts," "Left Hand, Right Hand," "Animals All Around," "Like Mexicans," "First Love," "Secrets," "Money," "Finding a Wife," "Going Back," "June," "Blue," "Waiting," "White Blossoms," "My Nephew," "On Our Own," "Taking Notice," "The Concert," "Canary, Cat, and Dog," "The Young Poet Under a Tree," "The Man on the Floor," "To Be a Man," "This Is Who We Are," "Expecting Friends," "Pulling a Cart," "This Man (2)," "Moving Around," "Listening Up," "One Thing After Another," "The Talking Heads," and "Saying Things."

From *Lesser Evils* (1988), I have included "The Girl on the Can of Peas," "Colors" (in a slightly different version), "This Man (1)," "Pets," "Evening Walk," "Dining in Fresno," "Ziggy," "Piedra," "Fire," "Moses," "Guess Work," and "Night Sitting."

Five recent essays are collected here for the first time. Grateful acknowledgment is made to the editors of the following periodicals and anthologies in which they were originally published: "Oranges and the Christmas Dog," *Las Christmas,* edited by Esmeralda Santiago and Joie Davidow (Alfred A. Knopf, 1998); "The Childhood Worries, or Why I Became a Writer," *The Iowa Review* (Spring / Summer, 1995); "The Effects of Knut Hamsun on a Fresno Boy," *El Andar* (Fall 1999); "Getting It Done," *Fathers and Daughters,* edited by DeWitt Henry and James Alan McPherson (Beacon Press, 1998); and "Who Is Your Reader?" *American Literary History* (Summer 1999).